THE MONEYCYCLE

Your Personal Journey to Financial Independence

DR. KAREN TOTTEN WHITE

ISBN: 978-1-7166-3247-1 (sc)
ISBN: 978-1-7165-7247-0 (e)

Scripture quotations taken from the New American Standard Bible® (NASB),
Copyright © 1960, 1962, 1963, 1968, 1971, 1972, 1973,
1975, 1977, 1995 by The Lockman Foundation
Used by permission. www.Lockman.org

Any people depicted in stock imagery provided by Getty Images are models, and such images are being used for illustrative purposes only.
Certain stock imagery © Getty Images.

Lulu Publishing Services rev. date: 10/16/2020

DEDICATION

To my children Roderick and Kristen.
Thank you for supporting me through this journey.

PREFACE

Over my thirty plus years of working in the financial industry, I quickly learned it rarely matters how much money individuals earn. Instead, the important fact is to understand how to manage what we earn. I have encountered some individuals with large salaries. The more they earn, the more they spend digging themselves deeper into the dangers of debt. I have encountered others who seemed to barely have any money. Yet they managed to live within their means making their resources last from pay-check-to-paycheck with extra to spare.

The MoneyCycle *is* a tool to provide financial wisdom, life lessons, assessments, and experiences from individuals who took the time to share their knowledge. The MoneyCycle *is not* a get rich quick gimmick. Inside, the MoneyCycle reveals methods to resolve financial issues which need to be addressed in order to take the journey to financial independence. The rest is up to you. Be persistent. Read and apply the techniques you learn and you will improve your financial position as well as accomplish your goals. Whatever level of knowledge you have in personal finances, you can start where you are to progress to where you want to go. I hope you enjoy your journey.

ACKNOWLEDGMENT

Many thanks to my family whom I love dearly, and friends who believed in me and inspired me. A special thanks to the following individuals: Dr. Rev. Alvin Edwards, Phyllis Holly Hankins, Dr. Lovell A. Maxwell, Reveda Merritt, and Wanda Owen for providing insight and positive criticism on the manuscript. Above all, to the Great Almighty for leading me through this process.

INTRODUCTION

You are traveling to a new destination in life-Financial Independence. The MoneyCycle is designed to help you map your journey to financial independence. The fastest route might be the highway, yet it is more costly because of tolls. The longer route might be through the city. You will have more stoplights, yet you will travel fewer miles. Warning! Whichever route you select, the journey is rarely smooth. The roads have potholes and manholes. The sun will shine, the rain will pour, the clouds will linger, the lighting will flash, and the thunder will roar. It's called life; the inevitable happens. Life might alter your route, but it will not deny your journey. Mapping your voyage provides tools to access your situation in order to adjust to life as it shifts gears along the way.

Financial literacy is simply financial education. How does this lack of personal financial education happen? Perhaps there is an assumption everyone naturally understands financial literacy. Maybe we believe the subject is being taught in the school system. Others may think the subject is personal, therefore it is being taught at home. Instead, we find personal financial education becomes a speed bump in our journey. We run over it before we realize it and get tossed around in the mishap. After hitting it, we just move on. But I believe there is a better way. The MoneyCycle is designed to help us correct any damage done in the past and prepare us with maintenance tips to assist us in our voyage to financial independence.

Topics such as "How to become wealthy," "How to get rich," or "How to become financially independent" were not taught in any of the schools I attended between kindergarten and twelfth grade. My teachers did a great job teaching Government, English, Biology, Math, History, Calculus, Trigonometry, and Geometry. Some of these classes were mandatory for me to graduate. Our goal is to graduate from high school and get a job. You work your way up in the company to be the construction manager, administrative assistant, or physical therapist. Perhaps you loved school and decided to go to college. After you graduate, you become a doctor, lawyer, engineer, chemical scientist, physician's assistant, paralegal, or another professional. You are doing excellent in your career and producing a generous salary. Yet, something is missing. You learned how to handle business for your industry, but did you ever have an opportunity to learn how to handle your personal financial business? If you are a Baby Boomer (born 1946-1964), Generation X (born 1965-1984), or Millennial (1984-1996), you may not have been privileged to personal financial training. Or perhaps the one day you missed class was the one day your teacher discussed "How to become wealthy," "How to get rich," or "How to become financially independent." Now is the time to treat ourselves to a financial refresher on the lost lesson from the one day we missed class. This will liberate us to move forward to the healthy place we desire to be with our finances.

So, right here, right now, let your journey begin! The MoneyCycle provides you with a personal SSP (Strategic Spending Plan) to assist you guide your hard-earned cash in the direction to benefit you the most. Imagine yourself driving on the highway at sixty miles per hour. The speed limit sign reads fifty-five, so you feel like you are within a safe range. Yet, as you look around everyone is passing by you. Suddenly, you feel like you are driving forty-five miles per hour on the same highway. What does this have to do with your financial journey? Everything! Always remember, everyone's journey is different, just like your financial situation. You can learn from another person's journey, but unless they are driving your vehicle or paying your debts, then you stay in your lane and maintain control of your financial situation. The main point is to start your journey and travel at a pace that works with your lifestyle. Following the steps in this book will help you to understand where you stand with your current financial situation, help you determine where you want to be in the future and assist you to create a personal SSP to guide you on a journey to financial independence.

The goal is to discover various methods to gain financial stability. This concept embodies the values of creating financial-awareness and having a forward-thinking mindset. Jump on the MoneyCycle to begin your journey to financial independence.

CONTENTS

CHAPTER 1

FINANCIAL FITNESS

The Physique of Finances

When the human physique is in agony, pain, overweight, or underweight some individuals immediately play the role of "Dr. Home Remedy" or "Coach Work It Out Myself." If Dr. Remedy and Coach Myself's techniques do not work, a decision needs to be made to call on a professional for advice. Being financially healthy is similar, it is about making appropriate financial choices. A decision-making process must occur. After this, actions must be taken to rectify the situation to relieve pain and get the physique back into a healthy condition.

Generally, when you go to the doctor, it is for a specific purpose. You may not feel well and need medical advice. You may be there for a follow-up visit from a prior checkup or you may be there for a routine preventive maintenance checkup. Like the fear of dealing with finances, some individuals have the "white coat syndrome." The white coat syndrome is when you get nervous merely thinking about going to the doctor. As a result, your heart starts to race as if you just completed a 5K marathon. Your hands feel damp with sweat as if you washed them yet the air dryer on the wall is not blowing hard enough to dry them. Your blood pressure skyrockets into infinity from fear of the unknown. You feel all these emotions at the same time even though the doctor may not have entered the room yet. Similar to this scenario, you will survive the overwhelming feeling of your financial concerns. You have already proven your determination by making a decision to start your journey on the MoneyCycle.

1

To remain physically fit, we often consult with professionals such as doctors, dieticians, nutritionists, coaches, and personal trainers who can guide us through our journey. When it comes to financial literacy, many of us simply don't know what to ask, where to go, or who to consult. This scenario can happen to a family member, a neighbor, a coworker, or it might even be you. At times, we may even feel embarrassed about our financial condition. If this is the case, we may not want to discuss the situation with anyone. But there is good news. You are not alone and you don't need to feel embarrassed or fearful.

Similar to how you might feel when talking with the doctor about a medical issue, talking with a professional about excessive or delinquent obligations can be quite emotional. The first step is to make the appointment to speak with a financial counselor. From there, many of us face a series of challenges. As we wait for the counselor to enter the room, our chest might get tight. It is easy to believe they will judge, thinking you must be an irresponsible person. Many of us might even consider leaving before they come into the private room. We might feel as if the situation is hopeless, yet deep down, we know the issue must be addressed. After all, the fear of the unknown is the real issue. But, what if the scenario is different than the one in our minds. What if when the door opens a smiling face enters the room and says, "Hello, please tell me a little about what is going on, then we can work together to create a plan of action?" Once you start the process, the journey may not be an easy ride. But the reward of perseverance and persistence is the removal of a financial burden. We must not self-diagnose. Instead, we gain when we seek financial advice from trained individuals. They can assist us to determine the best path to take in resolving any financial issues and relieve tremendous pressures.

Break It Down! What Is Financial Fitness?

The goal of Financial Fitness is to educate and inspire individuals to sharpen their skills in money management, consumerism, and financial planning. This journey involves learning how to successfully manage your financial expenses. Money plays a critical role in our lives. Not having enough money impacts our health as well as our intellectual performance.

To become financially fit, we must first define our financial goals, and then create a financial workout plan to accomplish each goal. There is good news. The information in this guide will increase your knowledge. Applying the knowledge you gain will improve your financial situation.

Pain Relief -Decreasing Debt

If your monthly expenses are more than your net income, the physique of finances will be in agony or pain. The results? Choices must be made immediately. Excessive debt can be mentally and emotionally stressful. It is the essence of being financially unhealthy. If we find ourselves in this position, it is crucial for us to evaluate our debt to find out what expenses can be decreased or eliminated. We must ask ourselves the following question before we make a purchase, "Do I really need it, or do I just want it?" As we think twice before making any purchases, we have opportunities to regain our financial health.

The reduction of debt decreases a portion of stress in our lives. This occurs as we take action to reduce our obligations. In the same way, we consume pain medication to relieve a headache, we must take action to eliminate our debt. It doesn't work if we buy the aspirin but leave it in the cabinet. To relieve your headache, the medication must be taken as directed. If the pain is persistent, it requires consistency to alleviate it. Sometimes, this means taking one tablet every four hours or taking three pills three times a day. In the same manner, we can use this simple plan of consistency with any debt we desire to eliminate. The first step is to confirm the balance. Next, we divide it by six, nine, or twelve, etc. depending on the amount. Then we can make payment arrangements with the creditor. This confirms our intent to pay a specific amount on a stated date until the obligation is paid in full. Finally, we make payments on time, faithfully each month. Have you ever noticed a warning label on the side of a medicine bottle? They often advise us to "Take this medication as directed." The warning label for financial pain relief reads: "Excessive Debt is Stressful."

> *It is better that you should not vow than that you should vow and not pay.*
>
> (Ecclesiastes 5:5, NASB)

The Financial Workout Routine

Now is the time to start a workout routine to build a healthy, financial physique. You are on your way as you set a goal for savings accounts, plan for investment accounts, and begin to work towards your plan. Many of us need financial physical therapy to sculpt our financial figures into shape. The next few pages will begin our financial workout routine to strengthen your financial condition as much as you desire, according to your level of commitment. We begin with you creating a self-payment plan or emergency fund. A self-payment plan is a specific amount deposited consistently into a savings plan. To start, open a savings account. Next, add deposits in constant intervals. Start small and increase your deposits every 90 days. If your payday is every other Friday, faithfully set an amount to be deposited into the "pay yourself account." The goal is to possess a money market, certificate of deposit and savings account for liquid assets in your financial portfolio. Next, you will develop your financial physique by adding mutual funds, stocks, bonds, and real estate to your portfolio. The overall goal is to decrease your debts, increase your savings, and work toward investing as you build your Strategic Spending Plan. We will elaborate on this plan in chapter 5.

We might be tempted to say: "Oh, I don't have enough money to save." or "After I pay my bills, there is not any money left." Yet, I find we often don't save because we simply do not have a plan in place. Having a plan is what helps us to meet our goals. It is not about how much we save; it is about training ourselves to get in a habit of saving consistently. Once you decide how much to save by a certain date or how much to save each pay period, put your goal in writing. Keep this written goal visible and review it weekly. Remember your savings account is your money. Think of it as paying yourself. It is an investment in yourself. To start meeting this goal, ask the Human Resource (HR) manager to divide your direct deposit. They can deposit a portion of your wages into your savings account each pay period. If the HR manager cannot honor your request, check with your bank representative to find out what opinions are available for saving plans. If your company provides a 401K plan, it is imperative to participate. If you do not, in five years you might look back and not even know where you spent the money you did not invest. If you do participate, you will feel a sense of financial security. This happens as you see how your dollars have grown over five years. Online tools like CalculatorSoup* can assist you in reaching your savings and investment goals.

*CalculatorSoup, *https://www.calculatorsoup.com* - Online Calculators

Savings versus Investments Key Differences

Savings are defined as a set aside portion of your income, intended for future use. On the other hand, investments are defined as opportunities to generate returns over a period of time. Savings accounts have little to no risk. Investing, on the other hand, includes a risk of losing money.

Savings Versus Investing

Savings (Insured)	Investing (Not Insured)
Greater Access-Lower Interest Rate	Limited Access-Higher Interest Rate
Savings Account	MMF-Money Market Fund
MMA-Money Market Account	MF-Mutual Fund
CD-Certificate of Deposit	

We begin on a path to financial health when we set an amount of how much we want to start saving and how often we will allocate funds towards our goal. If we do not start somewhere, we will end up nowhere. We must begin a plan of action to see results. This book will serve as a basic guide to develop a Strategic Spending Plan (SSP). In our time together, you will personalize the SSP by using your information. As you enter your data into the appropriate fields, your personal SSP will come together. This will allow your journey to move forward on the MoneyCycle towards financial independence. The steps along the journey include:

Write It! Write down the amount of your goal. This gives you a visual.
Read It! Place it where you can see it. This allows you to read it every day.
Believe It! You must believe in yourself. Know that I believe in you.

Record the vision. And inscribe it on tablets, that the one who reads it may run. For the vision is yet for the appointed time; it hastens toward the goal and it will not fail. Though it tarries, wait for it; for it will certainly come, it will not delay.

(Habakkuk 2:2-3, NASB)

Emergency Funds

Everyone faces situations in their lives when they need extra money. Instead of worrying about how, where, or who to get the money from, we can put ourselves in a financially healthy position so we can borrow the money from our own personal bank account. This is called an *emergency fund.* Essentially, this is a stash of cash set aside to cover the financial surprises life will toss your way. These unexpected events, such as sudden unemployment or medical catastrophes are stressful and costly. Implementing an emergency fund helps us to be prepared.

Party With Me People

The parable of the prodigal son (Luke 15:11-20, NASB) reveals a case of a young man who was emotionally unhealthy, he was unhappy with his lifestyle. This led to him being financially unhealthy. Financial stress can cause emotional distress. Likewise, emotional stress can cause financial distress. In this parable, the son decided he would leave his home and his family to explore a more exciting lifestyle. Like so many individuals who desire to take this step, the question is, "how would he fund his adventure?" The son decides to ask his father for his inheritance. He had one older brother; therefore, the son would receive approximately one-third of the estate.

According to the Hebrew Laws, families were required to pass their land and inheritance down the lineage in a specific order to preserve generational wealth. Yet, this young man decided he wanted what he thought was rightfully his. And, he wanted it now. Against the standard order of the Law, the father complied and honored his son's request. What was the result? The young man took the money and ran. Settling in a city nearby, he began to squander his inheritance. In essence, he launched his version of a Hebrew Celebration. He lived large, spending money like the pouring rain, faster than it could grow on trees- if that were even possible. The prodigal son had a New Year's Eve Time Square Celebration. He gained a lot of acquaintances and they graciously abetted him in spending his wealth. Undisputedly, he was "The Man of the Hour." Then, deprivation struck the land. The celebration came to an end. As his wealth faded away, so did his newly found groupies. He was having a New Year's Eve Time Square Celebration without generating revenue to replenish his expenditures. As the acquaintances decreased, the young man's emotional stress increased.

The prodigal son rode the MoneyCycle without using a SSP. He thought traveling to the other side the grass would always be green, the sky would always be blue, and everyone would regard him with higher esteem. Then reality set in. He had no money, no place to live, and the acquaintances he had moved on looking for their next victim. The prodigal son was at his lowest point. He hit rock bottom. He realized he needed to make some decisions; he chose to go home. The young man was disrespectful to his family and the Mosaic Law by leaving home. He returned knowing he could be scolded, or even put to death for his disrespectful actions. When the father realized his son had returned home, he welcomed him back home and celebrated the fact his child was safe.

The prodigal son believed his inheritance and wealth would make him happy. He thought he would be able to live the life he deserved. Instead, he wasted the finances given to him. After he experienced what it was like to be destitute, then he realized he had left a blessed life behind. The prodigal son had a quick fix in fame and fortune which left him in a bankrupt position. What can we discover from this parable? Though he was down, he did not stay down. He thought about his family, home, and former lifestyle. He swallowed his pride and went home to rectify the situation with the individuals who truly loved and cared for him.

We all have encountered a Prodigal Son at some point in our lifetime. This individual seems like they have everything, yet they are careless with their possessions. Maybe it's your neighbor, your friend, your family member, your parents, or your child. Could it possibly be you? And if it is you, it is okay. I believe you are in a spot to begin working towards healing to become financially healthy. Just like the prodigal son went to his father to make their relationship right, we have the same opportunity to correct situations with the people we encounter.

We have an opportunity to make wise decisions with your finances. There are several steps we can take to begin. To start, think about the individuals around you. Consider selecting someone who is a wise manager of their finances and ask them to give you a few pointers. Next, chat with a financial advisor, banker, or an older family member. If you cannot think of anyone around you to seek advice from, it's time to broaden your circle of acquaintances and consider asking someone you know indirectly.

Twenty-First Century Takeaway From The Prodigal Son:

1. **You have "free will" to make choices regarding your life.** It is important to pray and seek wise advice. The Prodigal Son made his choices without seeking wise advice.
2. **You must be willing to be accountable for your final decisions.** Whether they are right or wrong. The Prodigal Son realized he was in a terrible situation. Yet he came to his senses, he realized he did not have to stay in a terrible situation.
3. **If you make a mistake-- and you will-- it's not the end of the world.** Assess the situation and adjust accordingly to correct it. If you are not sure how to correct your situation, ask for help. The Prodigal Son chose to move back to a place of security where he was truly loved.
4. **Try not to dwell in the situation.** It is important for you to forgive yourself. This allows you to move forward with your life. The Prodigal Son was remorseful, yet he removed himself from the negative situation. This freedom allowed him to move forward with his life. You can do the same, move forward with your journey.

Stop spending money you don't have,
to buy the stuff you don't need,
to impress people who don't care!

Gaining And Retaining Generational Wealth

The generational wealth gap must be eliminated. This allows you, your family, and future generations to truly prosper. According to Nasdaq.com, more than 70% of families lose their wealth by the second generation. Usually, the generation who created wealth made many sacrifices and acted with great discipline. Sometimes I hear the comment, "I want my children to have more than I had growing up," or "I want my children to have what their friends have so they will fit in." Building generational wealth is not about purchasing the new, in-demand tennis shoes, the latest designer dress, or a car you can make a payment on but cannot afford to maintain. Understanding this concept, however, can be difficult to instill in others. The lack of training, understanding, and application causes the wealth gap to grow wider from generation to generation in some families.

If the generations before you were not in a strong financial position to share an inheritance, let the legacy begin with you. You can be the trailblazer in your family. You can be the game-changer who builds the foundation for passing down a significant inheritance to your future generations. Generational wealth is building on the financial success of past generations. Let it begin with you!

Let's continue the MoneyCycle journey to financial independence. Learning and applying diverse techniques will increase your financial stability. This concept embodies the values of creating financial-awareness and having a forward-thinking mindset. Here are eight easy tips to protect your money and build generational wealth over the long term. Implementing these simple tips will take your journey to the next level:

1. Seek financial advisers who can help you maximize your investments while minimizing risk.
2. Invest in your personal growth. Take a class. Go to seminars. Read financial books.
3. Build an adequate emergency fund. Strive to save three to six months of your living expenses.
4. Setup automated deposits to your savings and investment accounts.
5. Review your accounts at least once every quarter. Increase your deposits to your savings and investment accounts quarterly.

6. Shop around for high paying interest rates.
7. Avoid late credit card or bank fees.
8. Set up automatic transfers to purchase stock in small intervals to build yourself a portfolio.

Generational wealth consists of assets that can be passed down or inherited from generation to generation. Examples of these assets include:

➢ *Cash:* checking accounts, savings accounts, and certificate of deposits.
➢ *Investments:* stocks, bonds, and mutual funds.
➢ *Real Estate:* houses, land, rental property, and intellectual property
➢ *Business Ownership:* franchise, and small business.
➢ *Collectibles:* antiques, toys, stamps, wine, artwork, comic books, and coins, etc.

Notice this list does not include the latest name brand tennis shoes, designer dress, or a car you cannot afford to repair if it breaks down. Some items are simply necessary to survive in life. Other items are not essential. You might like the item, but purchasing it is not an investment. How do you know what is and is not an investment? Take an inventory of what you currently possess. Do you have a foundation to build generational wealth? If you do, good for you! If you are not sure, it's time to make a few honest adjustments to position yourself and your family for future financial security. Take a minute to review the list again, celebrate if you have accomplished any of the tips on the list. From this point, determine which tips you would like to accomplish as you move forward with setting goals.

Symptoms of Unhealthy Finances

According to Prosperity Now, millions of Americans would encounter lifestyle hardships if they miss only one paycheck. The report found 40% of American households are "liquid asset poor." This means they don't have enough money in an account to make ends meet if their income is unexpectedly interrupted.

I will not buy what I cannot afford
I will choose "Long-term Prosperity"
Over "Short-term Pleasure"

Prescriptions For Financial Fitness

The answer to financial fitness is not a one-size-fits-all. If the doctor gives us several prescriptions at one time, some medications might state "take if needed." Some may instruct us to take once a day, others may instruct us to take twice a day. In a similar manner, the next step for us to progress in our financial journey is to use one or more of the prescriptions to put ourselves in a healthier financial position according to our personal needs. Remember, our financial health will affect our mental and physical health.

I encourage each of you to continue to reach out to someone for help. There are individuals who love and care for you. There are also individuals who are highly trained in financial matters, who can see through any obstacles you might feel are overwhelming. Trust me, there are individuals waiting to pour advice, knowledge, and love into your life. Look around you. Whether these individuals are friends, family, mentors, coaches, leaders, or coworkers, there is someone willing to assist you to be the best person you can be emotionally and financially. In return, "each one should teach one" by sharing the knowledge gained. When individuals take time to pour advice, knowledge, and love into your life, pay it forward by sharing the information with others. If you look around and see someone going through a hard financial situation, try to provide them with guidance and encouragement. Refer them to organizations that might be able to assist them. We can all work together toward financial fitness.

Contact the Federal Trade Commission for basic Consumer Information at https://www.consumer.ftc.gov/. Contact the Consumer Financial Protection Bureau for financial questions regarding banks, lenders, and other financial institutions to make sure that you are being treated fairly at https://www.consumerfinance.gov/. We are moving towards happy, healthy, healing financial goals.

A Financial Affair

Throughout my thirty-plus years' career in the financial industry, I held many positions. A Bank Teller, Customer Service Representative, Mortgage Loan Officer, Business-to-Business collector, Branch Manager, Assistant Vice President/Managing Officer and Regional Lending Manager just to name a few. In the role of AVP and *Managing* Officer, my responsibilities included growing the operations of two branches, employee training and retention, and ensuring compliance. The role of *Officer* provided me with lending authority to grow the bank's loan portfolio.

When I began to train within the loan department, one of the senior lenders said to me, "Don't be an order taker. This is not the Burger Barn, it's the bank. The customer cannot always have it their way." He made it clear it was my job to listen to the customer, find out what they needed, and create a solution that would be a good fit for their request. Yet, I needed to accomplish this without putting the bank at risk with the dollar amount of the loan. This required interviewing the loan applicant through general conversation, gathering all financial data to understand as much personal information as possible.

One of my faithful customers referred (we will call them) Ella and Greg, new clients, to me for a business loan. I met with Ella. After listening to her request, I quickly realized the challenges we needed to tackle. She said they needed to borrow $15,000 to free up working capital for their business. I provided her with a list of the standard documents the bank would require to process a loan. The list consisted of:

Personal Information

- Identification for verification.
- Personal assets.
- Personal liabilities.
- Tax returns if separate from the business.

Business Information

- Business background information.
- Business plan.

- Credit references.
- Tax returns.
- Business assets.
- Business liabilities.

If the loan was approved, I would need additional information. This included but was not limited to:

- Business license.
- Articles of incorporation.
- Leases for rent rolls.
- Contracts with third parties such as clients and vendors.

We set an appointment for Ella and Greg to return with the requested information. I cleared my schedule with great anticipation. The couple returned and I started the application. The process seems to be moving along nicely until I pulled their personal credit report to verify their current debts and payment history. We needed to determine:

- Can the customer afford the new loan payment?
- Are the balances on the credit report correct?
- Are the payments being made on time? If not, why?
- Does the debt belong to the applicant? If not, who does the debt belong to?
- If the debt belongs to someone else, who is making the payment?
- Can the customer afford the payment if the other person does not?

A credit report and tax returns can expose undisclosed information to a loan officer or credit analyst. This is a vital step since individuals tend to omit certain data either in error or on purpose. The result of gathering this information is to determine if the customer can afford the new loan payment.

I started a dialogue with the couple to share my findings. "The credit report shows a high credit of $6,000 and a balance of $5,895 owed to Belk-Leggett, is that correct?" Greg facial expression immediately changed. He looked like I had backhandedly slapped him. I felt the tension enter the room like a windstorm coming through the door of my office. Greg proudly said, "We don't have a credit card with Belk-Leggett." Ella cordially reached over to massage Greg's leg to calm his inward brewing wind storm. She spoke in a soothing voice, "Honey, I had to charge a few things for the kids." Then she looked at me, "That is correct. It is my bill for the children." I continued, "The reports also show a high credit of $5,000 and a balance of $4,624 owed to Old Navy, is that correct?" The cycle repeated itself. Greg leaned forward in his chair. The windstorm in his gut resurfaced. This time he looked at me as if I double smacked him with a backhanded slap. His voice drops into a deep baritone. With a slow firmness, he said, "I know we do not have a credit card with Old Navy." Again, Ella cordiality extends her hand to massage Greg's leg to calm his internal fermenting windstorm. In the same comforting voice, she said, "Honey, I needed to charge a few things for the grandchildren." She looked directly into my eyes as she spoke, "That is correct. I shop there for my grandchildren." This continued approximately three more times before Greg decided he could not handle it anymore.

He essentially discovered Ella had been unfaithful to him with credit cards. I had become the detective banker who exposed the spending affair. He felt the windstorm move from his gut up his esophagus into his mind. He must have thought to himself, "What else is she doing that I don't know about?" "Are we about to lose our business?" Does she have any other accounts the banker hasn't told me about?" "The children and grandchildren are not in desperate need of anything. Why is Ella spending so much money on them?" "Why did she have these credit cards and not tell me about them?" "She is spending all of this money and it's not even Christmas!" Greg has sunk into a deep silence. He grew numb to the fact that Ella was massaging his leg. He finally broke the silence, "Thank you for your help. We need to look at a few things before we decide what we need to do."

I was a little embarrassed to be the one who exposed Ella's financial affair with credit cards. However, this was part of my investigative duties as a loan officer. It was my job to stay unbiased, follow the procedure, and ensure each customer was treated fair and with respect. Two options were available- loan denial or loan approval. Loan denial required justification. This occurred if we proved the client's income could not support the new loan payment. This meant the loan was a high risk for the bank.

Loan approval required justification that a clients' income could support the new payment. Yet, if a loan became delinquent, it would become my responsibility to provide financial counseling for the client to assist them in getting the loan back on track. I was not able to approve Ella and Greg's loan request. It would have been a high-risk loan for the bank. I suggested they increase their rental income by 3% when they renewed leases on their commercial tenants, re-evaluate their vendors to decrease business expenses, eliminate the unnecessary credit card debt, and decrease personal expenses. These actions would require some discipline for their personal and business lifestyle. The good news is they were receptive to the suggested solutions and their marriage did survive the financial affair.

The Symptoms And The Solution

As a result of feeling stressed from the business which encompassed so much of their lives, Ella became a victim of emotional spending. This resulted in her buying items she did not need and eventually could not afford. Many of us may have experienced stress which led to emotional spending. Are you a victim of emotional spending? Consider these indicators:

Symptoms - Emotional Expenditure

1. Shopping has become a response to stress.
2. Spending has become "keeping up with the Jones'."
3. You seek the high of instant gratification.
4. You tell yourself you deserve it.
5. You are spending, yet you are worried about money.
6. You are shopping with intent to return items.
7. You justify a want, not a need.

Solution – Healing Emotional Spending

1. Speaking: Pray before you pay.
2. Shopping: Confront your feelings.
3. Seeking: Identify your emotional spending triggers.
4. Shopping: Set a budget for the "I just want it" purchases.

5. Seeking: Ask for help, find an accountability partner.
6. Shopping: Find alternative activities. Read or volunteer your time.
7. Speaking: Say it out loud in the mirror, "I will be healed of emotional spending."

Finding The Right Fit For Financial Fitness

Check with your service providers to determine if you have the proper accounts to meet your financial needs for your lifestyle.

Ask yourself:

A. What are your personal financial needs?
B. What services are provided at no charge?
C. Do they charge monthly fees?
D. Do they provide options to avoid fees?
E. Can you afford the fee?

Bank Accounts:

1. Open a "Household Account" for monthly bills.
2. Open an "Expense Account" using a debit card for personal expenditures.
3. Open a "Saving Account" for emergencies.

Investment Accounts:

1. Individual Retirement Account-IRA.
2. Certificate of Deposit-CD.
3. Mutual Fund.
4. Stocks.

Insurance:

1. Health Insurance.
2. Life Insurance.

3. Homeowners Insurance.
4. Renters Insurance.
5. Auto Insurance.

Credit Report Check-up points:

Get your free annual credit report to verify the debts on the report belong to you. If they do not belong to you or they look suspicious, file a dispute. It will cost you time, but it is better to correct it before you apply for credit and get an unwanted surprise. For your free annual credit report logon to www.annualcreditreport.com.

Mini Module:

The Inventory List

Based on the information regarding generational wealth, develop an inventory list of your current possessions that can be considered an asset.

1.

2.

3.

4.

5.

6.

7.

8.

9.

10.

The Financial Fitness Check-Up

Keep in mind, there are no good or bad scores. Your interpretation will depend on the goals you set for yourself based on your values and needs. We will discuss the purpose of some of the following questions in more detail as we move through the MoneyCycle. Now, let's steer into the questions?

1. Do you currently have a personal budget, spending plan, or financial plan?

   ☐ Not at all   Assign 0 point
   ☐ Somewhat of a plan   Assign 3 point
   ☐ An active pan   Assign 5 point

2. How confident are you in your ability to achieve a financial goal you set for yourself?

   ☐ Not at all confident   Assign 0 point
   ☐ Somewhat confident   Assign 3 point
   ☐ Very confident   Assign 5 point

3. If you had an unexpected expense or someone in your family lost a job, got sick, or had another emergency_____, how confident are you that you could come up with the money to pay your bills for three months?

   ☐ Not at all confident   Assign 0 point
   ☐ Somewhat confident   Assign 3 point
   ☐ Very confident   Assign 5 point

4. Do you currently have an automatic deposit or electronic transfer set up to put money away for future use (such as savings)?

   ☐ Yes   Assign 5 point
   ☐ No   Assign 0 point

5. Over the past month, would you say your spending on living expenses was less than your total income?

   ☐ Yes   Assign 5 point
   ☐ No   Assign 0 point

6. In the past three months, have you been charged a late fee on a credit card, or any bill?

   ☐ Yes   Assign 0 point
   ☐ No   Assign 5 point

7. Do you have a checking account?

   ☐ Yes   Assign 5 point
   ☐ No   Assign 0 point

8. Do you have a savings account?

   ☐ Yes   Assign 5 point
   ☐ No   Assign 0 point

9. Do you have an emergency fund account with 1-6 months of cash in savings?

   ☐ Yes   Assign 5 point
   ☐ No   Assign 0 point

10. Do you have an investment fund account with stocks, bonds, mutual funds, etc.?

   ☐ Yes   Assign 5 point
   ☐ No   Assign 0 point

11. Do you have an individual retirement account to be accessed after age 59½?

- ☐ Yes   Assign 5 point
- ☐ No   Assign 0 point

12. Do you know your net worth?

- ☐ Yes   Assign 5 point
- ☐ No   Assign 0 point

13. Are you paying all bills on time each month?

- ☐ Yes   Assign 5 point
- ☐ No   Assign 0 point

14. Do you know your credit score?

- ☐ Yes   Assign 5 point
- ☐ No   Assign 0 point

15. Do you have health insurance?

- ☐ Yes   Assign 5 point
- ☐ No   Assign 0 point

16. Do you have homeowners or renter's insurance?

- ☐ Yes   Assign 5 point
- ☐ No   Assign 0 point

17. Do you have auto insurance?

- ☐ Yes   Assign 5 point
- ☐ No   Assign 0 point

18. Do you have life insurance?

    ☐ Yes   Assign 5 point

    ☐ No   Assign 0 point

19. Do you have a dedicated money space to pay your bills and keep important documents?

    ☐ A dedicated space   Assign 5 point

    ☐ Somewhat of a space Assign 3 point

    ☐ Not at all   Assign 0 point

20. Do you have beneficiaries named on your accounts?

    ☐ Yes   Assign 5 point

    ☐ No   Assign 0 point

Total your points:

75 or above indicates a strong financial condition.

74-35 indicates areas which need to be reinforced.

34 or below indicates weakness which can be strengthened with a plan.

Your baseline score can be improved by implementing the Strategic Spending Plan in chapter 5 of the MoneyCycle. Try answering the questions to the Financial Fitness Check-Up again. Do the module 90 days after you complete the guide to measure your improvement. Next, plan to follow-up with a third checkup 180 days from the first date of your Financial Fitness Check-Up. Strive to improve your score by 25 points every 90-days. If you take action, you will see positive results.

Score   Date

_____   _____ Today

_____   _____ 90 days

_____   _____ 180 days

"Becoming financially healthy leads to becoming financially wealthy!"

Dr. Karen Totten White

CHAPTER 2

INVESTING IN YOURSELF

Lessons For Life

For the first thirteen years of my life, I was the only grandchild in my mom's family. They treated me like a little princess. My grandma (Momma) and my mom's sister (Auntie) adorned me in cute little play dresses with matching hair bows, sandals, or tennis shoes and lace socks. They even dressed me up just to go outside and play with a selected group of children. The chosen playmates and the princess played games like hopscotch, red-light green-light, and hide and seek. Also, they allowed me to take a few toys outside. This included a jump rope, bolo bat, hula hoop, and jack rocks.

Auntie faithfully took me to Sunday school and church every Sunday. At six-years old, I didn't quite understand the purpose of the church service, but I could tell it was a major event in our weekly routine. Auntie decorated me in beautiful, frilly dresses with matching lace socks, and patent leather shoes. The Sunday morning service was a big deal in the community. This meant wearing the proper attire was non-negotiable. On Easter Sunday, my attire was expanded with lace gloves, a tiny purse, and a matching hat with a ribbon dangling from the back. Sunday school was especially fun because I learned biblical stories in a manner that I could understand. The big thrill was sitting at a little wooden table with matching little wooden chairs small enough for my six-year old little body. After Sunday school, we went upstairs to attend the morning church service. The massive edifice, Loyal Baptist Church, was built 1923-1924. It could seat one thousand people at capacity. I was filled with amazement and reverence whenever I entered the grand edifice. Mr. Alexander Owen sat proudly in the balcony as he played the morning prelude on the golden pipe organ. Our pastor, Rev. Dr. Doyle J. Thomas Sr., was a well-respected, civil rights leader. He was a pillar of the community.

I knew I needed to be on my best behavior as the usher escorted me to the dark hardwood theater chairs. It was the beginning of my etiquette lessons. I had no choice but to sit up holding my back straight, legs crossed at the ankle, and hands crossed, resting on my lap. I would stand when others stood and sit when others sat unless I was directed to do otherwise. At six-years old, I did not understand everything happening during the service, but I did always understand the proper manner to sit and stand. I needed to pay attention. Why? Because at any time during the service, Rev. Thomas' voice would echo throughout the sanctuary in a happy manner. He would come down from the pulpit, sit at the baby grand piano, sing a happy song, and the entire congregation would join in. Every man, woman, boy, and girl were dressed in their Sunday best outfit. Everyone appeared to be happy and having a grand time as we sang the songs of Zion, clapped our hands, patted our feet, and swayed from side-to-side. I did not waiver from the protocol, I joined in with the happy celebration. It felt like a warm, sunny day with a cool breeze flowing inside the building.

What did I learn? If you want to play, then you have to pay. The privilege of attending Sunday school and sitting in the little wooden chair came with a sacrifice. Subsequently, I had to attend the morning service and sit in the big, hardwood theater chair. Auntie always made sure I had dimes, quarters, and a dollar for the Sunday school and morning service offerings. She taught me to invest in the mission if I truly wanted to be vested in the organization. She taught me the importance of generosity, responsibility, duty, and commitment. The ladies and gentlemen of Loyal taught me church protocol. The atmosphere was regal and I understood that it was of great importance to those who attended. The lessons they taught demonstrated their reverence for the Lord and their commitment to mentor the younger generation. They took the time to invest in me.

Fast forward ten years. At sixteen years old, I got my first job as a salesperson at a locally owned business, Gunnies Jean. My Papa taught me to spend within my means and always save money by paying myself. He believed it was okay to spend some money, but not to run out of money before you could replenish your supply. He taught me at an early age not to spend or give away my hard-earned $3.10 minimum wage hourly pay. He taught me to save a percentage of my income because life's events would happen. They always do. With this guidance, I learned to be ready for unexpected circumstances. Momma, Auntie, Papa, Mom, and my family invested in me. They instilled values which taught me to carry myself with pride. Why? Because there is only one of me and they were proud of me. They showed me they loved me and taught me to love myself. They taught me a direct relationship between my intrinsic value and my investments. They invested in me and taught me to invest in myself.

> *For where your treasure is, there your heart will be also.*
> (Matthew 6:21, NASB)

Fast forward another ten years. I began my career in the financial industry. I provided excellent customer service for clients to ensure their financial success. I was a team player who motivated others to get the job done and accomplish their stated goals. The ending result was financial success for the company. Because of my dedication, the clients respected me. I developed a great relationship with my supervisors and coworkers. Day-in, day-out, the same process. Why? Because I wanted to invest in a mission that I believed in.

Through this pattern, I became a crew member for everyone else's MoneyCycle. There was a problem with the pattern, I lost track of my own personal business for the future. I began to observe the individuals around me in the financial industry. I realized I needed to move forward in the MoneyCycle journey. Some of my coworkers began purchasing stock when it became available. I believed I could not afford the stock, so I held myself back. Some of my coworkers had certificates of deposit. I did not think I could afford to purchase the long-term investments, so again- I did not invest. On certain occasions, my coworkers would have a business partner bid on and purchase the bank's repossessed real estate. It seemed risky and I did not think I could afford to purchase the investment properties. But, was it true? The common denominator in each scenario was the fact "I thought I could not accomplish the challenge." No one told me I could not, I just assumed I could not. Assuming is a dangerous action. I needed a change of mindset and this is exactly what happened.

I decided to start small, I purchased a one-year certificate of deposit. I learned how to shop around for the best rate when the C.D. matured. A coworker disclosed that a customer wanted to sell some stock. I asked her to add my name to the list of potential investors. Then, I acquired some stock. With time and research, I began to learn about real estate investments and property management. After two years of homework, I found an equitable deal and I had become financially stable enough to make the acquisition. As I completed my doctoral degree, everyone began to ask, "What are you going to do special to celebrate your major accomplishment, take a cruise, or go to the beach?" I replied, "No, I purchased myself an investment property!" To this day, it is one of the best presents I ever purchased for myself.

Even though I worked in the financial industry, I had to learn how to invest in myself on a larger financial level. When I thought I could not afford what everyone else had, then I could not. When I decided I could afford the investments, then I studied and asked questions to determine how to obtain what I desired. I reached another level of learning how to invest in myself. It is an ongoing quest. I'm still learning how to take care of my MoneyCycle as I move through the journey.

Investing in yourself is a learned process. Starting small and being consistent will help you to be successful. Comparable to the triumphant race between the tortoise and the hare, it's not about who finishes the race first. The victory is found in staying in the race until you reach your stated goal. It's about stating a goal, determining what you need to do to make it happen, and moving forward. It's about assessing your current situation and adjusting to position yourself for prosperity and wealth in the near future.

The life lessons I have learned include:

- The people who truly love and care for you will invest in your well-being.
- Learn whatever you can from those who invest in you and be grateful you had an opportunity to connect with them.

- There are other individuals who you will encounter who will be the opposite.
- Learn whatever you can from those who do not invest in you and be grateful you had an opportunity to disconnect from them.

Break It Down! What Is Investing In Yourself?

To invest in yourself means to invest in your future. Material things come and go, but your knowledge stays with you. By investing in a coach or a trainer, you learn new things. Thus, you are empowered with knowledge. According to the Huffington Post, investing in yourself is one of the best returns on investments you can ever have. Whether it's investing by learning new skills, developing yourself personally or professionally, tapping into your creativity, or hiring a life coach – it all matters. Investing in yourself will position you mentally, physically, and financially to invest in others.

Preparation Is The Name Of The Game

The Parable of the Ten Virgins (Matthew 25:1-13, NASB) displays the importance of investing in yourself. The virgins traveled on the same journey and each took their oil lamps. There was only one difference between them. The five wise virgins took extra oil to add to their lamps. The five foolish virgins only had the oil that was in their lamps. As they traveled on their journey the oil became low for all ten virgins. The wise virgins were prepared because they had extra oil to refill their lamps. Yet, the foolish virgins had none. Instead, they asked the wise virgins to share their oil. The wise virgins refused because they realized it would put them at a disadvantage. They were wise enough to realize two possibilities. First, the probability was great that they would run out of oil themselves. Second, the foolish virgins were not mentally prepared for the event.

Investing in yourself is not about being selfish, it's about self-care.

The ten virgins knew to expect an event to occur even though they did not know when to expect the event. There are a few topics to consider in this parable. First, we cannot help others until we are in the proper position to help them. On an airplane, the flight attendant provides instructions for the passengers, they always state "In case of an emergency, put the mask on yourself first, then put it on the other passenger." Next, we must understand the fact -- we cannot help everyone. If you consistently help individuals who are not trying to help themselves, you will eventually cause a hardship for yourself. As the old saying goes "Birds of the same feather flock together." Think about it, enabling is different from helping. The virgins in the parable all had the same opportunity. Yet, five were proactive and five were reactive. Think about the company you keep. Would you say you are part of the five wise or part of the five foolish? Are you proactive or reactive in most of life's situations? Are you an individual with a backup plan or without a backup plan? No matter where you find yourself, we all have room for improvement. How does this parable relate to you investing in yourself?

Twenty-First Century Takeaway From The Parable Of The Ten Virgins:

1. **You cannot give what you do not have to give.** You cannot help everyone. You are not the Salvation Army or the Red Cross. There is a process to get assistance from these organizations. If you receive request frequently, then refer them to the Salvation Army or the Red Cross. This allows you to provide solutions without depleting your resources.

2. **It's okay to say "No."** Learn to discern the difference between guilt and conviction. If you feel guilty, pray before you say *"no in a loving way."* If you feel conviction, pray before you say *"yes in a loving way."* I call it "spiritual blackmail" when people manipulate you into doing something which will be harmful to you in the future. It's okay to just say, *"No."*

3. **Be prepared.** It is up to you to use your resources wisely. If you have an income -- whether it's self-employment, a career, social security, disability, retirement, investment funds or whatever -- it

is up to you to be a wise steward with your resources. No matter how small or large.

4. **If you fall prey to undesired situations, use the situation as a lesson.** This prevents repetitive undesired situations. Have you ever run out of gas? It happens. Yet, it should not continue to happen habitually. Has your debit or credit card ever been declined? It happens. Yet, it should not continue to happen regularly. Have you ever been late for work? It happens. Who hasn't from time-to-time? Once again, it should not happen frequently.

Thinking Outside Of The Box

According to a survey from Bankrate, which interviewed 1,003 adults, fifty-seven percent of Americans don't have enough cash to cover a $500 unexpected expense. It is pivotal for us to prepare ourselves for life's expected and unexpected events by persistently saving. This can be accomplished in small, medium, large, or in any amount -- weekly or monthly. Pay yourself consistently, just as if you are paying a bill. You earned the money, you pay everyone else, pay yourself! This will put you in a positive financial position to help others without leaving yourself in a detrimental financial position.

Preparation is an imperative part of starting your MoneyCycle towards financial independence. This guide will provide you with the knowledge to boost yourself into the driver seat, take control of your finances, and begin your journey. In addition to having money in the savings or investments, think outside of the box for additional resources you can use to support your lifestyle and future needs. Keep in mind, some resources may not be financial. These are your community resources such as:

- Friends, family, or entrepreneurs who can help you make wise financial decisions.
- Community services offering public transportation options, education centers, job training, or cultural events.

- Schools, hospitals, churches, libraries, or recreational centers providing free or reduced-cost clinics, childcare, education, and training.
- Work benefits such as life insurance policies, legal help, identity-theft protection, or health programs offering rewards for positive behaviors.
- Anyone you know who can provide connections to credible advice and expertise you may need.

Here Today! Gone Tomorrow!

The changes in life's circumstances can impact your lifecycle on different levels. These circumstances vary according to if we are unprepared, somewhat prepared, or prepared. Preparation is a key factor for investing in yourself. Knowing how to handle situations will decrease stress levels. The loss of income or the loss of a loved one can both have a major impact on our lifestyle. These events can change our financial situation in the blink of an eye. Both events can be emotionally devastating as well as financially tragic. In the following examples, preparation can make a difference in the short-term and long-term of your situation. Knowledge is power.

Loss Of Income

You are not alone. You are not the first person who has experienced this misfortune, nor will you be the last. It can be very hard to discuss this type of loss, but it is imperative for you to reach out to someone you can trust. If you have not done so before, now is the time to look at methods to invest in yourself. The loss of employment or a business venture is only as devastating as we allow it to be. We must remember to not let the situation control us. We must control the situation. Let's discuss a few methods of preparation to consider before, during and after a loss:

Preparation For Loss Of Income		
Before	**During**	**After**
Invest in an emergency fund.	Give yourself time to grieve	Replenish your emergency fund
Update your resume and keep your skills up-to-date. Spend within your limits.	Think of the loss as a temporary setback	Update your resume with your new skills and position
Think about your skills and how you can monetize your skills.	Express your feeling with creative methods	Think about the skills you need to improve on or learn more about and work towards learning them.
Network to build new connections.	Network to build new employment.	Network to build new relationships.
Join a career website. Keep your skills up-to-date.	Stay connected with career websites and job clubs.	Update your skills on career websites and job clubs.
Volunteer.	Volunteer.	Volunteer.
Communicate with your loved ones.	Communicate with your loved ones.	Communicate with your loved ones.
Never get too comfortable with your job.	Most people will not know unless you tell them what happened. Let them know your job was phased out and keep it moving.	Continue to be grateful for your new career.

Loss Of A Loved One

It is important to have a conversation to discuss the possibilities. Let your loved one know your desire to follow their wishes. If it is too hard to discuss, ask your loved one to leave all important documents in a specific location with notes. Let's discuss a few methods of preparation to consider before, during and after a loss:

Preparation For Loss Of A Loved One		
Before	**During**	**After**
Take time to prepare. Invest in life insurance.	Give yourself time to grieve.	Give yourself time to heal.
Discuss where to locate important documents.	Handle the business at hand	Keep all documents in a central file for tax purposes.
Prepare an inventory sheet to list debts, account numbers and contact information of creditors.	Allow your friends to be there for you.	Notify the three credit bureaus to prevent identity theft.
Discuss your wishes with each other. Make sure their wishes are made clear.	During your vulnerable time, have a trusted individual to assist you with the business decisions.	Update mailing addresses with the USPS and other important contacts.
Think about how you want people to remember your loved one so they can leave a loving legacy.	Follow the instructions your loved one left on record for you.	Set up an estate account bank account to distribute assets and handle ongoing expenses.
Communicate with your loved ones.	When people ask what they can do, give them something to do. Perhaps they could cook a meal, run an errand, assist with notifying others, or vacuum the floor. Contact an organization to let them know of the loss.	Be grateful for the time you shared with your loved one. Cherish the memories.

Changing Routes

Several years ago, I met a middle-aged lady named (let's call her) Ava. She owned a residential cleaning business. The business provided her with a good income. One day I asked her what made her decide to start her business. I was not prepared for her response. Ava told me she had been a waitress in a chain restaurant. She made good tips and was happy with her job. Her father passed during the holiday season so she took time off to handle the arrangements. Her boss responded in a very insensitive and thoughtless manner. Dealing with the unexpected death of her father, Ava needed additional time off after the services to resolve his personal business. When she requested the additional time off, her boss told her she was no longer needed. She was fired! It was a double whammy. Yet, Ava turned her situation around and changed the route of her journey. Working smart to blaze a trail, she became an entrepreneur with a lucrative cleaning business. Ava prefers to operate on a small scale, she said she actually had to turndown new clients from time-to-time. As I listened to her story, it was inspiring for me to learn how she turned around the situation that she was able to control. Even after losing her primary income and her loved one, Ava invested in herself by changing the direction of her journey.

Techniques To Invest In Yourself

1. **Honor your instinct.** Trust your instinct, and go with your gut feeling. Honor the hunch it is sending you. As you listen to your intuition, you will have the opportunity to make logical decisions. Even when you seek advice, the decision you make is the decision you will have to deal with and face at the end of the journey. Your influencer may or may not be available after your final decision is in action. It is important to know what empowers you to stay on track. I encourage you to pay attention to your surroundings. This will help you to make healthier and more shrewd decisions. Ask for guidance, but trust your intuition. At the end of the journey, you will be solely responsible for the outcome of your decisions.

Some will be right and some will be wrong. The benefit to each of us is the fact we can learn a new lesson either way.

2. **Invest in building your self-confidence.** Individuals who know their worth speak words of encouragement and others pay attention. Invest in yourself by expanding your understanding of your value. Offer this same insight to the individuals you encounter. Continue to speak the truth, love, and encouragement to people in your life. The more you love yourself and endorse the value you offer, the more confident you will be in sharing your inspirations with others.

3. **Health is wealth.** Think before you eat. Plan your meals. Drink water. You will feel better and have more energy. Exercise daily. Search for 15-30-minute workouts on YouTube. Walk up or down the steps instead of riding the elevator. Do something every day to get moving and get your heart rate up, even, if it's just walking to the mailbox. Exercise gives you the energy to take on the day with confidence because of how it makes you look and feel. It is an extremely important part of this journey. Wealth means nothing without your health!

4. **Invest time in your creativeness.** We all have unique skills. Have you discovered yours? What is your creative skill? You might be in your thirties, forties, fifties, or sixties before you discover what you want to do and what you are good at doing. Your skill will feel natural, yet you still work to master it. It is the ability you have on the inside which you share with others. Creativity can be a catalyst in the manifestation of continual learning and lifelong activities you share with others. It inspires you. In turn, you share it to inspire others. With a healthy investment of creativeness, your skill can become your commodity. With a precise investment of time, your commodity can be sold on the open market.

5. **Invest in a coach.** A life, career, financial, personal, or health and wellness coach can assist you in putting your plans into action. A coach can be your escort to success. It is their goal to assist you to accomplish your goals.

6. **Read informative articles and books.** Constant learning allows you to become a well-rounded individual. Articles, blogs, and

books are splendid methods to develop your knowledge and expertise in whatever area you desire. Knowledge of a subject matter will allow you to contribute a little to a conversation, while listening will allow you to learn even more.

7. **Attend seminars and symposiums**. Develop your current skills, knowledge, and abilities in your business and/or personal life whenever you have an opportunity. Networking in this manner will allow you the opportunity to interact with like-minded individuals who are heading where you want to go.

8. **Set your goals.** Learn how to set personal and business goals for yourself. The old cliché states *"if you fail to plan, then you plan to fail."* You need to know where you are going before you start the journey. Even if you change directions along the way, you should have a general idea of where you want to go and what you would like to accomplish. Value your time, it is precious. Set reasonable timelines to achieve your personal and business goals. Consider the **S.M.A.R.T.** goals approach -Specific, Measurable, Attainable, Relevant and Timely.

I can promise this: When you invest in yourself, a world of opportunities will open for you.

Investing in yourself emotionally, physically, spiritually, and financially, allows you to become the best version of yourself. When you are the best version of yourself, you are a resource of inspiration to others!

Mini Module

Invest in Yourself Exercise: S.M.A.R.T. Goals

Today's Date: _____   Start Date: _____

Target Date: _____   Date Achieved: _____

This process will assist you to identify your S.M.A.R.T. Goals. Then you will create a path to accomplish your stated goals. When writing your S.M.A.R.T. Goals, use brief statements with pertinent information. Think about what you want to accomplish to improve your current lifestyle. It's for you and about you. Smile, think positive, and expect to succeed!

Initial Goal *(Write your objectives)*:

_____

_____

_____

1. **Specific** *(What do you want to accomplish? Who needs to be included in your journey? When do you want to complete this? Why is this a goal?)*

_____

_____

_____

2. **Measurable** *(How can you measure progress and know if you have successfully met your goal?)*:

_____

_____

_____

3. **Achievable** *(Do you have the skills required to achieve the goal? If not, can you obtain them? What is the motivation for reaching this goal?)*:

_____

_____

_____

4. **Relevant** *(Why am I setting this goal now? Is it aligned with overall objectives?)*:

_____
_____
_____

5. **Time-Bound** *(What is the deadline and is it realistic?)*:

_____
_____
_____

S.M.A.R.T. Goal *(Evaluate your answers written above. Now, create a new, more focused goal statement based on the answers disclosed in the questions above)*:

_____
_____
_____

This Goal Is Important Because:

_____
_____
_____

The Benefits Of Achieving This Goal Will Be:

_____
_____
_____

Take Action!

Potential Obstacles   Potential Solutions

_____   _____
_____   _____
_____   _____
_____   _____
_____   _____
_____   _____

Who Will You Ask To Help You?

_____

_____

_____

Specific Action Steps: *What steps need to be taken to reach your goal?*

Goal	Expected Start	Completion
_____	_____	_____
_____	_____	_____
_____	_____	_____
_____	_____	_____
_____	_____	_____

And all things you ask in prayer, believing, you will receive.
(Matthew 21:22, NASB)

How Are You Investing In Yourself?

Use the chart below to determine if you are actively investing in yourself.

Learning From Others

➤ As you go through life, networking in the right circles can impact--
your income as well as your social status. Some people talk a great talk,
yet it is clear there is no action behind their words. This group teaches
us 'what not to do.' If it looks like a duck, for right now, -- it's a duck.
Connect yourself with people who have proven to be a game-changer
in life. To begin, think of an individual who appears to have their
financial affairs in order. Next, ask them to share their number one
success tip with you. Continue the journey by making a list of people
who you admire. Ask these individuals to share their stories about their
success or ask one specific question to generate a conversation. Take
notes and listen, listen, listen!

Individual	Success Tip
✓ _____	_____
✓ _____	_____
✓ _____	_____
✓ _____	_____
✓ _____	_____
✓ _____	_____

Investing In Others

➤ Remember, when you discover what works for you, share what you
have learned with anyone willing to listen. This is helpful, especially
with children and young people in your family. An individual is never
too young to learn basic financial tips. This is how we can contribute to
decreasing the generational wealth gap. Make a list of younger people
who you can mentor.

	Individual	Success Tip
✓	_____	_____
✓	_____	_____
✓	_____	_____
✓	_____	_____
✓	_____	_____
✓	_____	_____

Investing In Yourself Is Powerful

Investing in yourself delivers a powerful message. Look in the mirror or use the camera on your cell phone. Read this empowerment message out loud to yourself:

I am valuable. I possess the potential to succeed at whatever I attempt. There is only one of me. I add value to society. Therefore, what is invested in me, I will share with others to create positive results in their life. I am important.

CHAPTER 3

MONEY MANAGEMENT

Green Peas And Bumble Bees

I magine spilling a bowl of green peas on the kitchen floor. You see it happen in slow motion right before your eyes, but there is nothing you can do to prevent the inevitable event. The peas fly out of the bowl like baby bumble bees bouncing through the air. Then, they just flock to the floor rolling around aimlessly. Stunned, you stand there looking at the remaining seven spoonsful of peas that did not escape from the bowl. Feeling a little disgusted, you place your Corelle bowl on the kitchen counter. You get the broom and dustpan from the laundry room to sweep up the flyaway peas. As you sweep ten peas towards the dustpan, four of them roll to the right. A small victory, you succeeded to get six peas in the dustpan. Then, you reach back to get the four that rolled away. As you pull the broom towards the dustpan, one pea rolls the left. You feel like you are playing a green pea bumble bee video game that you do not have time to play nor do you want to play. Finally, you sweep up the last pea and empty the dustpan into the trashcan. Victory! You gained ten points playing the green pea bumble bee video game. Now for the grand prize, you get to relax and enjoy eating the peas that did not escape.

Controlling debt can be like chasing green pea bumble bees flying in the air. It takes several attempts to resolve issues. This can happen fast, yet we feel as if we are watching the aftermath in slow motion. Sweeping the peas from the floor is like clearing delinquent debts from a credit report. Sometimes a delinquent debt will post on a credit report before you can intercede, similar to peas hitting the floor before you can catch them. When small and large issues are resolved, we feel better mentally, our credit score soars in an upward direction, and we find ourselves in a better financial position. Applying the techniques in the MoneyCycle will guide you through the process to reach your desired resolutions.

Managing money is a topic we may not want to think about. At times, it even causes stress. CNBC news surveyed 1,000 U.S. adults who encountered financial stress. The results, 85 percent say they "sometimes" feel stressed about money, and 30 percent say they're "constantly" stressed about their finances. Know you are not alone in your journey. Regardless of how much or how little money we utilize, from time-to-time we must deal with the details. Comparable to sweeping up spilled green peas, we know we need to tackle the issue. As we know, leaving peas on the floor only creates a messy, unsafe situation. The same is true when money is improperly managed.

Throughout the MoneyCycle, we will work on tackling issues together using multiple methods in this guide. If you feel money management is stressful, following this roadmap will improve your confidence and im-prove your money management skills. It is imperative for us to properly manage our current funds, the small gestures count. This includes paying debts on time and working to reduce or eliminate debt. One of the most important tips is to pay yourself by implementing an emergency fund.

We might ask the question, "How can I do all of this at the same time?" It is possible with a plan. The goal is to map out a strategic plan. Next, we travel at a steady speed to reach the destination. The average trip from Virginia to California is 2645 miles. This takes 40 hours, not including stops. There will be various obstacles such as paying tolls, stop-ping for gas, checking the oil, stopping for food, and stopping to rest. It is not a fast journey. But it is a grand tour to enjoy as you see your progress along the route. The journey to establish healthy money management skills is similar. The most uncomfortable part of the MoneyCycle may be getting your current spending and future savings in-line with your current income. The MoneyCycle can be hard or easy, let's work together to make it easy. Taking the journey one mile at a time allows you to measure your progress. Remember to celebrate your small milestones, as well as the large milestones. You are on the right track!

Break It Down! What Is Money Management?

Money management includes the practice of budgeting, saving, investing, spending or otherwise managing the wealth of an individual or group. Money management can also be referred to as investment management and portfolio management. You might think, "I don't have any money to manage." This is not true. Beginning small is the key to early successful money management skills. If you have one dollar, and you manage it properly, you can multiply it. Having a forward-thinking mindset when it comes to money management allows your journey to be a positive challenge.

Double or Nothing!

The Parable of the Talents (Matthew 25: 4-28, NASB) reveals an example of how individuals manage money differently. The parable reveals how the Owner is going on a journey. In his absence, he entrusts a certain amount of money or talents to each worker. The Owner assigns five talents to the first worker, two talents to the second worker, and one talent to the third worker. The workers are challenged with being wise stewards by managing the money until the Owner returns. When the owner returns, the first worker has doubled his money, now he has ten talents. Likewise, the second worker has doubled his money, now he has four talents. The third worker, however, was afraid of taking a risk. Instead, he chose to do nothing with the money left in his possession. He maintained the same one talent. The parable tells us the Owner was pleased with the first two workers because they made wise decisions with their money by investing the funds to generate income. The Owner was displeased with the third worker because he did not make an effort to make good use of the money. He took the one talent from the third worker and gave it to the first worker who earned the most with his investment.

This ancient parable is comparable to the modern-day reality television show - The Apprentice. The reality show judges the business skills of the contestants. The show features fourteen to eighteen business-minded individuals who compete for business deals. One contestant is removed through the process of elimination at the end of each episode. Contestants are divided into two corporations or teams. One member from each team volunteers as the project manager for each new assignment. The teams compete in business-related tasks such as selling products, raising money for charity, or creating an advertising campaign. The winning team is selected based on objective measures and subjective opinions of the judges and advisors who monitor the teams' performance. The losing team attends a boardroom meeting for the show's host and their advisors to explain why they lost and determine who contributed the least to the team. Each episode ends with the host eliminating one contestant from the competition with the notorious words, "You're fired!" The remaining contestants compete for the show's prize, a one-year $250,000 contract.

At times, life feels a lot like a parable or a reality show. We see individuals who have the most continuing to gain more, while the individuals who have the least stay in the same position. It is normal for us to desire more money. Yet, it is imperative for us to be wise stewards with the funds we currently manage. Whether you can relate to the first, second, third worker, or the Apprentice team, improving your money management skills will improve your financial position. Let's continue the journey for you to transition closer to financial independence.

Twenty-First Century Take-Away From The Parable Of The Talents:

1. **This parable explains how success is a result of our work.** We were made to work. The book of Genesis reveals Adam's duty was to cultivate and care for the garden. We also have a mission to accomplish. We are called to work using our gifts to serve the common good of mankind. Using biblical principles will assist us to be successful by working diligently with our skills to the best of our abilities. Are you using the talents entrusted to you wisely?

2. **The parable explains how we are provided with everything we need to accomplish our vocation.** In the New Testament, a talent was a large sum of money. We are expected to generate a return on investment by using our talents towards productive ends. The

worker who was given the least received what he could manage. He was provided with enough to produce more. Yet, he chose to bury his gift. What talent or money have you buried, wasted, or misused?

3. **The parable explains how we are not all created equal.** The Owner gave each worker talents "according to their ability." The worker who received one talent produced exactly what he generated and the owner was wise enough to realize this in advance. It would have taken the same amount of work for the one talent worker to double his money as it did for the other two workers. Yet, everyone is not willing to put in the work to get the results. Are you willing to put in the work to be successful?

4. **The parable explains the fact we should work for excellence and not for egotistical purposes.** The workers are the stewards of the Owner's investment. It is the quality of their stewardship the Owner is measuring when he reviews their work. We should work in excellence, using our gifts to promote positivity, and growth in everything we do. We can succeed. Are you a wise steward with the responsibilities you handle for others?

5. **The parable demonstrates how we will be held responsible for our actions.** It also provides examples of how we can work to fulfill our earthly calling. We are called to embrace whole-life stewardship. The unfaithful worker wasted his opportunity. We are responsible for what we do with what we have been given. Therefore, we must strive to be well-rounded in our spiritual, physical, mental, and financial life.

Can you think of a time you wasted an opportunity? Do you ever say "If I had this, then I could do that?" What type of worker are you? Which amount do you think the Owner would entrust to you today? Can you make savvy business decisions to benefit a team or company?

> *"How you spend your time and use your talent will determine how you spend your money."*
> Dr. Karen Totten White

Money Managing Mindset For Success

Money management begins with having the right mindset. According to MSN Money, 70% of lottery winners will file bankruptcy within 5 to 7 years of winning. Money management is about properly managing your funds and creating residual income. If money is spent and not replaced (like the lottery winner) or it is spent faster than it comes in (like a paycheck), then changing your mindset needs to occur so your spending habits will change.

During my tenure in the financial world, I encountered a customer who won a sizable lottery. The first mistake, it was announced in the newspaper. The second mistake, the couple went on a shopping spree. The third mistake, the couple did not seek financial advice. Since they were not familiar with managing money at that level, it would have benefited them to hire a financial adviser. In the end, the couple had more debt than they started with. Sadly, their relationship dissolved in a divorce.

How well do you manage your money—whether the amount is large or small? Applying the knowledge you gain from the MoneyCycle will empower you to manage your money instead of allowing your money to manage you. How you spend your time and use your talent determines how you spend your money. Maybe you are into baking, photography, genealogy, or archery. You may be a bowler, golfer, skydiver, swimmer, or hiker. This is where you use your talent and spend your time because it is what you (love) to do. How can you pay it forward using your time and talent to benefit others? Consider using your talent by teaching someone else your skills. You will continue to enhance your gift by using it by sharing your skills with others. If you are extremely skilled you might consider monetizing it. Determining how you are going to spend your time and use your talent is part of the money management process to prepare for your financial future.

Cutting Cost

Think about areas where you currently spend money. Which of these expenditures could you decrease so you can add the extra money into your emergency fund or investments? Implementing this strategy will cost you a minimum amount of time while saving you a maximum amount of money.

In the long run of the MoneyCycle journey, following this practice will increase your return on investments. Consider implementing a few of the cost-cutting tips below. Less than thirty minutes on the phone per call can save you hundreds of dollars per year.

Cut Subscription Cost

1. Shop around for the following providers' services to compare fees for cable, satellite, cell phones, and internet packages.
2. Purchase your modem and router instead of renting it from the provider.
3. Monitor your bills closely and question unexplained charges. Always feel free to ask what the purpose of the charge is and if it is required.
4. Ask the provider to remove unnecessary charges and request a credit for the current bill.
5. Keep a spreadsheet of comparable services of each competitors' prices when you are calling around requesting the best rate.

Cut Insurance Cost

1. Seek a multi-discount premium by combining auto, homeowner, or renter's insurance with the same provider.
2. If your premium continues to go up and you have not had any claims, shop around. Remind your agent of your good track record. This gives them the incentive to compete for your business.
3. If you have an emergency fund, increase your auto and homeowner, or renter's deductible from $500 to $1000. This will reduce your premium. Then, add the difference to your emergency fund.
4. Reduce your comprehensive and collision coverage to the minimum state law requirements for older automobiles.
5. Consider a Term Life policy. Work on increasing your investments to cover expenses before the term expires.

6. Contact your insurance agent before you purchase a vehicle to determine if the premium will exceed your budget combined with the new auto payment.

Cut Credit Card Cost

1. Select a credit card with no annual fee.
2. Monitor your statement for any unexplained charges or fees. Contact the company immediately if you do not understand a charge.
3. Shop around for cards with cashback and reward point options.
4. Use balance transfer options with no interest for 6-18 months.

Mind Your Personal Business

1. **Identify Where Your Money Is Going.**
   Be mindful of how you are spending your money. A $5 cup of coffee, five days a week costs you $100/month. Evaluate your purchases. Find the areas you can reduce spending and add the money to your savings account. Start by reducing regular spending habits or go cold turkey by eliminating spending in one specific area.

2. **Create A Strategic Spending Plan (S.S.P).**
   Plan for your expenditures by developing a budget and live within your means based on your monthly income. Assess your expenses and make adjustments to remain within your budget. Consider leaving your credit card at home to avoid spending shortfalls and unnecessary purchases.

3. **Incorporate Savings In Your S.S.P.**
   Pay yourself first. Pay yourself first. Pay yourself first. Handle your savings account like any other monthly bill by making a monthly payment to yourself. Start with a specific amount such as $50 per paycheck for three months. Then, increase your payment to $75 per paycheck. Increase your deposit every three months until you reach your desired goal for your savings account. Consistency is the key.

4. **Plan For Major Purchases.**

Adjust your budget appropriately to increase savings for your next major purchase to eliminate using credit. If you do use credit, search for credit cards with zero percent interest. Pay on your purchase monthly. This allows you to benefit from the interest-free promotion.

5. **Project For Emergencies.**

Most experts suggest having a minimum of six to eight months of your salary available in an emergency account. Although this goal can take time to achieve, remember you must start somewhere to get anywhere. Again, the key is to start and be consistent.

6. **Plan For Retirement.**

Take advantage of interest and market upturns by saving for retirement as early as possible. Most employers will offer a retirement benefit with a 401(k) plan. This method of savings allows you to benefit from pre-tax dollar by using payroll deduction.

7. **Get Tax Guidance.**

If you have circumstances that create tax quandaries (e.g., self-employed, own and/or lease property, real estate investments, etc.), make sure to seek tax guidance from a professional tax consultant and an attorney. What you do now can protect you for later.

8. **Safeguard Your Credit.**

Select a month, perhaps your birth month to retrieve your free credit report. Each reporting bureau grants consumers a free annual credit report. Go online to www.annualcreditreport.com to receive yours. Review the information for accuracy. If the report reflects a debt that looks suspicious, file a dispute. The dispute will result in the information on the report to be corrected and updated which benefits your credit score.

This will cost you a little time, but it is better to correct it before you get an unwanted surprise, apply for credit, or make a major purchase. In most cases, if your credit score is low, you will pay a higher interest rate on auto, home, and personal loans. If your credit score is high, you pay a lower interest rate on the same loan products.

9. Home Office.

Utilize online tools, as well as paper copies of receipts, keep records of your pay stubs, banking information, taxes, insurance, and other documents important to your financial situation. It's your personal business. Take good care of it. Select a dedicated money space in your home to take care of your personal business. Keep hard copies in a specific location. This allows you to find it when you need it.

10. Each One Teach One.

Teach your children, nieces, nephews, and young people you have an opportunity to mentor the financial lessons you learn. This includes the good, the bad, and the ugly. It is always good to learn what to do. It is also good to learn what not to do. Share your story, everyone has at least one.

Attitude Creates Altitude

As a child, I was not familiar with the term "lack." Was I rich? No. Was I wealthy? No. Was I poor? Maybe. If I was, I didn't know it. Why? Because from my perspective, I always had everything I needed. The village (my family) took care of me. My mother, Papa, dad, stepmother, grandmothers, aunts, uncles, great aunts, and great uncles, etc., were all a support system. My family tree went on and on. My village pulled together to make sure (our) needs were met. I was born during the last year of the baby boomers. I was very fortunate to grow up not having to deal with the term "lack." How did I skip the feeling of lack? My family operated as a unit who worked together. My great uncle brought sweet potatoes from his garden. My great aunt brought turnip greens from her garden. My Auntie, who raised me, loved to dress me up like a prized china doll.

What is the point? Each one can teach one. They taught me the importance of sharing excess resources to prevent the experience of lack in someone else's life. Sharing must be taught. Many of us will experience individuals who are only takers. My advice? If they cannot reciprocate sometime in some form, just move on. Your aim should be to share your gifts, talents, knowledge, or excess with someone. In return, they will share their gifts, talents, knowledge, or excess with you as well as others. The goal is to gain knowledge and reduce expenses for all parties involved. Sharing knowledge should never be taken for granted. The lack of knowledge is a strong contributor to poverty and generational wealth gaps. Be the first to start a positive domino effect with your family and friends to decrease or eliminate lack so the next generation will be in a more financially stable position.

> *"Your attitude about your finances will determine your altitude with your finances."*
> ***Dr. Karen Totten White***

In 1 Chronicles 4:10, NASB, we find a short prayer uttered by Jabez. He calls on the God of Israel saying, "Oh, Lord, bless me indeed and expand my territory." Jabez requested God to bless him greatly, exceedingly, or abundantly. He can provide beyond all you can ask or imagine. This is a highly recommended prayer request. Yet we should be mindful to properly manage what we are already responsible for before asking for more. Use your willpower to decrease the term "lack" in your vocabulary. How is this accomplished? It happens by living within your means and focusing on what you *do have* instead of what you *don't have.*

You can accomplish whatever you desire if you are generous with what you have, are willing to make some sacrifices, and put in the work to reach your goal. Do you have to be rich? No. Do you have to be wealthy? No. You must simply use wisdom when managing your current responsibilities. This is true whether it is sweet potatoes, turnip greens, or your MoneyCycle. Was my family rich? I don't know. Was my family wealthy? I don't know. Was my family poor? I don't know. What I do know is they were wise enough to survive by working together and they understood how to manage with the resources which were available to them. I believe in the concept my family taught me- be grateful and show gratitude. Therefore, I share the concept because I know it works. Be grateful for what you have, show gratitude for your knowledge by sharing it with others, and always seek to learn more. Make the Jabez prayer request:

Now Jabez called on the God of Israel, saying, "Oh that You would bless me indeed and enlarge my border, and that Your hand might be with me, and that You would keep me from harm that it may not pain me!" And God granted him what he requested.

(1 Chronicles 4:10, NASB)

Creating Residual Income

According to Investopedia in personal finance, *residual income* is the amount of income an individual has after the deduction of all personal debts and expenses are paid. Whether an individual's income is $50K per year or $250K per year, if their expenses are $50K and $250K respectively they are living paycheck to paycheck. The goal is always to increase your income while decreasing your debt. Let's discuss methods for increasing income by decreasing expenses to create residual income:

- ➢ **Take surveys**-Get paid. Earn shopping points for taking surveys, watching videos, and playing games at SwagBucks.com. Redeem points in cash or gift cards at major retail stores.
- ➢ **Sell on Amazon**. Sell items you no longer have a use for on Amazon.com.
- ➢ **Digitize your coupons**. The SnipSnap app stores digital coupons directly on your smartphone.
- ➢ **Small grocery cart**- choose a small shopping cart. This will limit the number of items you pick up. It will also help you to stay focused on needs versus wants.
- ➢ **Learn the pattern**. Grocery chains promote certain products at regular intervals. Your favorite ice cream might be offered "buy one get one" once a quarter. Treat yourself during that timeframe to reduce cost.
- ➢ **Eat out for less**. Go to restaurants when they offer the best deals. For example, $2 tacos on Taco Tuesday. Eat lunch by 2:00 pm or 3:00 pm before the daily lunch specials end.

- ➤ **Call before you pay.** Banks and credit card companies will usually waive certain fees if you are not a repeat offender. If you have an overdraft at the bank or a late fee on your credit card, call to request a fee waiver. Smile. Remind them you have been a good customer and you appreciate their assistance with your request.

Living Within

If you make $100k a year and you spend $101K, then you have excessed your budget. Below is a quick example of budgeting for success.

Income	Expenses	Budget
$100,000	$80,000	Under budget
$100,000	$100,000	Paycheck to paycheck
$100,000	$101,000	Over budget

Mini Module

Life Management Toolkit

➤ Learning the art of negotiation can save you a lot of money over the years. Negotiate everything. For instance, your cable service, internet service, interest rates on loans, interest rates on investments etc. Remember the stated price or rate is an "asking price" or a "proposed rate." There is generally more than one provider for a service. This gives you leverage to negotiate. They can only say "yes" or "no" to your request. Corporations want your business and so does someone else. List some of your service providers below. Which three can you contact to negotiate a better deal for yourself?

✓ _____
✓ _____
✓ _____
✓ _____
✓ _____
✓ _____

➤ Financial risk must be addressed by asking questions. "What is the worst scenario?" What are the advantages and disadvantages of the risk? Having the proper information decreases the risk of loss and increases the rate of return on investment. Call your insurance company to inquire about a lower premium and a higher deductible. Compare the risk before making any changes. Can you afford to pay the higher deductible to save on your premium?

✓ _____
✓ _____
✓ _____
✓ _____
✓ _____
✓ _____

➤ Working hard does not mean working 24/7. Working smart is the happy key. Good health is often the result of spending time with those we love. Additionally, working smart allow us to be social while our money is still working for us. List a few ways you are proficient in making your money work for you?

✓ _____
✓ _____
✓ _____
✓ _____
✓ _____
✓ _____

Where's The money?

Understanding how you manage your money is imperative to enhance your current financial position. Remember, you must know where you are in order to determine where you are going and how to get there. This mini-module will assist you in determining the direction of your personal journey on the MoneyCycle to financial independence. Writing down your answers will provide a clear picture for you.

1. What "needs" do you regularly spend on?

2. What "wants" do you regularly splurge on?

3. What do you splurge on even when money is tight?

4. What is the most expensive item you possess?

5. Are you taking steps to save more money?

6. What is the smartest financial decision you've made?

7. Can you repeat this process?

8. How do you feel about your salary?

9. What hobbies or skills can you monetize to increase your income?

10. What other financial goals would you still like to achieve?

CHAPTER 4

PLAN OF ACTION

The Knowing-Doing Gap

It's time to implement a Plan of Action. Let's take the information and tips discussed in the previous chapters and put them into action. Financial independence starts with a mindset. Therefore, the true definition has diverse meanings. For one person, it means having enough residual income to live on without working unless they desire to do so. To another person, it means paying their bills on time each month, having an emergency fund, some investment accounts, and being able to take a great vacation. These goals can certainly be attained by building a financial cushion, writing a financial plan, creating financial goals, living within your means, and following through with your stated plan. If you know what you desire to do, then it's time to make your vision a reality. The '*knowing-doing gap*' is the difference in knowing what to do and executing a plan of action. The MoneyCycle provides you with tools to execute a plan of action. Answering the questions within this guide are part of the maintenance you will experience on this journey. Remember, your answers will be unique to your current lifestyle. Yet, your unique answers will assist you to obtain a clear focus and path to create your desired lifestyle. To complete this journey, you will take action by following the steps, adding to the steps, and implementing the steps. As you determine what you need to do, you must take action for the process to be effective. Earlier you used the S.M.A.R.T. Goal exercise to record your personal goals and the steps needed to make them happen. Now, it is time to position yourself to obtain and maintain financial independence. Now that you know, let's go!

Break It Down! What Is A Plan Of Action?

A plan of action should align with your strategic objectives and the outcomes you desire to achieve. They include your Strategic Spending Plan (S.S.P). Yet, the implementation of the strategy starts with your objectives. An effective plan of action contains several small steps that you will achieve on the way to accomplishing your larger goal. The small steps allow you to see your progress along the journey as you successfully move towards your goal. Remember to celebrate your small milestones as well as the large milestones.

Work! Wealth! Win!

Lydia was one of the most successful business-women in the Bible. According to Acts 16:14-15, NASB, Lydia was a business-woman who colored and sold purple cloth. She specialized in a material used by the wealthy influential individuals of her era. Lydia had a nontraditional career in the textile industry marketing to a high-end clientele. The textile industry is predominantly concerned with the blueprint, manufacturing, and distribution of fiber, fabric, and apparel. Miuccia Bianchi Prada, Vera Wang, and Robyn Rihanna Fenty are modern-day examples of Lydia's clients. Lydia was more than just a woman who sold luxury goods to the influential and the powerful. Records indicate she was also the head of her household, an entrepreneur, an employer who created jobs, and a dedicated Christian. She was the first European to convert to Christianity and the first to establish a meeting place in her home for Christians to congregate.

Lydia is a great example of an individual who had a plan and put it into action. She discovered her gift and used her skills, knowledge, and abilities. She put her knowledge into action to provide for her family, create jobs for others, and meets a need for clients. In return, Lydia's actions created wealth. She was a great influence on the people around her. She was a game-changer who was not afraid to venture into the non-traditional textile market.

Perhaps you have an entrepreneurial spirit. Maybe you have a skill or gift that you can transform into a business. Perhaps it is your dream to transform a hobby into a part-time or full-time career. Let's take a few principles from Lydia's plan of action to determine how you can use your skills to create residual income, help others, develop a prosperous business, and become a successful entrepreneur.

Twenty-First Century Take-Away From Lydia The Entrepreneur:

1. **Operate with integrity in excellence**. Lydia took her responsibility as a business-woman seriously. One essential attribute for Christians is always to practice operating with integrity in excellence in all situations. We do not seek perfection, but we do pursue excellence. You can demonstrate biblical principles through your attitude, personality, and business decisions twenty-four hours a day, seven days a week.

2. **Start small, grow big**. Lydia was able to grow a successful business allowing her to hire employees. Growing a business means creating opportunities for others to enrich their livelihood. Entrepreneurship boosts the local economy, enhances your status, and escalates your influence as a business professional. Think about the people and positions you would like to add to your business as it grows. In the initial business planning stages, consider how and when you will start to hire a small workforce to expand your business operations. Refer to the Small Business Administration https://www.sba.gov/ to assist with a business plan or write your own.

3. **Develop a dynamic business**. Lydia was a no-nonsense business-woman who formed a major enterprise in a prosperous marketplace. If she did it, so can you! Small or large, your skills can add value to the economy. You have the potential to grow big. If you are pursuing big dreams, use Lydia as your role model to grow your business by developing your skill. Remember, "Yes, you can!"

4. **Attempt non-traditional opportunities**. Lydia's role as a wealthy merchant of purple cloth was a non-traditional business during her lifetime. Be open to learning, working, and operating in any industry. Step out of your comfort zone to explore non-traditional

business opportunities. Be the trailblazer. Consider creating new avenues to success by exploring non-traditional careers.

5. **Be gracious in your daily endeavors**. Lydia opened her home to have worship services for others during an era when the church was a new concept. Always keep your priorities in line. Remember you are an ambassador for God. Always make sure prayer is part of the agenda for your business.

6. **Work/life balance**. Lydia managed her household as well as operating a successful business. You must find your personal methods to manage your work/life balance. Maintaining a home and operating a business can be challenging, but it can be done. Just think, Lydia didn't have access to the internet or a cell phone. If she did it then, you can do it now. Ask for advice from the successful people around you. Spend money to outsource certain tasks to give yourself some downtime in your personal life.

7. **Succeed in your prosperity**. Lydia gives us confirmation that Christians can be extremely successful and prosperous. A biblical principle Christians should follow is to build businesses that honor God, as well as gain a profit with a purpose. Remember to be generous and operate in philanthropy with your prosperous life.

"Our **Purpose** will enable us to become successful.
Our **Success** will enable us to become prosperous.
Our **Prosperity** will enable us to fulfill our purpose."
Dr. Karen Totten White

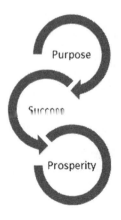

Willing, Able, And Ready!

Lydia started her journey on the MoneyCycle to financial independence and continued to the next level-wealth. She was a game-changer. She was a visionary who altered a business strategy and developed a nontraditional career as a merchant. She positioned herself to use different business strategies to compete directly and indirectly with her competitors. Lydia was a woman with a plan who put her plans into action. What talents, skills, and gifts are inside of you which you can share in the marketplace to make a profit? Perhaps everyone loves the aroma of your food. Consider a catering business, becoming a personal chef, or selling your goodies to local stores. Perhaps you have a strong willpower to workout. Consider teaching exercise classes, yoga, Zumba classes, or becoming a personal trainer. Perhaps you are really health conscious. Consider creating a nutrition plan, or publishing a healthy cookbook.

If you have an eye for style and fashion, consider opening an online boutique or being a fashion consultant. If you love the smell of burning rubber, consider a delivery service or teaching student driving classes. If you are bilingual, consider teaching an English as a second language (ESL) tutoring service. If you are good at cleaning, consider operating a janitorial business and contracting with businesses, the local, state or the federal government.

Look around the next time you are riding on a main street, highway, or boulevard. Every business you see started with someone who learned to monetize their talent, skill, or gift by transforming their thoughts into a reality. What sets these individuals apart is the knowing-doing gap. It started with a thought or idea. Next, they developed a plan. They put the plan into action to create what you see when you ride by or visit the establishment to purchase their products or services. Turn your talent, skills, and gifts into multiple streams of income. There is no time like the present to put your thoughts into a plan and your plan into action.

He has filled them with skills to perform every work of an engraver and of a designer and of an embroiderer, in blue and in purple and in scarlet material, and in fine linen, and of a weaver, as performers of every work and makers of designs.
(Exodus 35:35, NASB)

The Compass Of Entrepreneurship

Maggie Lena Walker was the first woman and the first African-American to found and become the president of a chartered bank in the United States. She was born into poverty on July 15, 1864, in Richmond, Virginia. At the age of 14, Walker volunteered for the Order of St. Luke, a mutual aid society which provided financial and educational support to African-Americans in need.

As an entrepreneur, Walker founded the St. Luke Herald newspaper, the St. Luke Emporium, and the St. Luke Penny Savings Bank. She later became chairman of the board of the Consolidated Bank and Trust Company. Maggie did not have a cell phone, the internet, an email address, or Google. She was a trailblazer, game-changer, wife, mother, and businesswoman. Maggie Lena Walker was a woman with a plan and she put her plans into action. (https://mlwgs.com/welcome-to-mlwgs/maggie-lena-walker/)

Whimper Or Have Wine

It was a cloudy morning in January. The brisk, cold breeze line danced to perfection with the rain as it gently dripped from the sky. It was a dreary day on the outside, but my heart was racing with excitement on the inside as I traveled to the Grow Your Sales Conference sponsored by the Virginia Department of SBSD (Small Business and Supplier Diversity). At the time, I was in the process of obtaining my SWaM (Small, Women-owned, and Minority-owned) certification. Therefore, I attempted to attend each seminar the SBSD offered. My goal was to enhance my entrepreneurial skills. As the informative breakout sessions came to an end, the SBSD allowed three veteran entrepreneurs to share their journey with the newbies. Gwen Hurt began to share her adventure of how she had everything going for her. She had three great kids and a prosperous career in Information Technology which afforded her to globetrot on business trips. This life was far removed from the poverty of her childhood. She reflected on her early days stating she and her siblings each had one pair of shoes to wear for the entire year!

Then, Gwen's life took an unexpected turn. She was released from the job she loved after giving over 15 years of her life to the company when they downsized. As Gwen and her daughter Brittny traveled to pick up her personal items from the office, a car crashed into theirs. The accident left them both severely injured. Gwen stated, "The doctors gave us a choice, surgery which provided no guarantee or one year of physical therapy." They choose the one year of physical therapy to recover from their injuries.

As Gwen recuperated, she refused to give in to depression. She said she opened the curtain one day to let the sunlight come into the room. She got her walker and moved into the hallway. She said to Brittny, "I'm going to start my own wine business." Brittny replied, "What kind of pain medication did they give you? I need some of what you have."

Gwen put her thoughts into a plan of action with a business idea she had over prior years. She turned her wine-making hobby into a business. Through her international travel, Gwen had developed a deep appreciation for fine wines. Brittny suggested she name her wine creation after something she loved. Gwen was crazy about shoes. That day *Shoe Crazy Wine* was born! Gwen was a woman with a plan and she put her plan into action.

As I entered the conference that cloudy January morning, the weather was cold and dreary. The brisk cool breeze line danced to perfection with the rain as it gently dripped from the sky. As I left the conference that afternoon, the rain, and clouds had dissipated. The cold, brisk breeze line danced to perfection with the bright sunshine in the sky. It was beautiful outside. My heart raced with excitement as I drove away. I was inspired to continue my journey into entrepreneurship.

Entrepreneurial Express: The Business Of Business

An overview of the steps to starting your business.

1. **Research your market.**

   a. Who are your competitors?
   b. Is there a demand for your product/service?
   c. Will people pay for your product/service?

2. **Create your business plan.** This is your roadmap to guide you through the necessary steps. Examples can be found online at https://www.sba.gov/business-guide/plan-your-business/write-your-business-plan#section-header-2 or you can draft your own.

3. **Select your business name.** Think about a name that captures your brand, products, and services. Pick a name that stands out and be remembered.

4. **Select a business structure.** Select one or more of the following:

    a. Sole proprietorship
    b. Partnership
    c. Limited liability company (LLC),
    d. Corporation (C corp., S corp. B corp., Close corporation)
    e. Nonprofit corporation

5. **Register your business.** Register with federal, state, and local agencies to protect your business name.

6. **Obtain your federal and state tax ID numbers.** Apply for your business ID numbers to keep the identity separate from your personal assets.

7. **Obtain your licenses and permits.** There are different requirements according to your state, city, and local government. This is another good reason to have a business plan, it will help you to stay organized by keeping this information in one location.

8. **Obtain your business bank account.** Shop around for a bank that caters to small businesses. This will help to keep your maintenance fees low on the front end of your start-up business.

9. **Finance your business.** Be prepared to put some of your personal money towards your business venture. As a former banker, one of the first two questions you will be asked is, "How much will this business cost?" and "How much cash do you have to put up for the venture?" You are investing in yourself, your future, and in creating generational wealth. Be prepared to invest your cash before you ask others. Some methods for raising capital are:

    a. Personal savings
    b. Bank loans

c. SBA loans www.sba.gov
d. Business credit cards
e. Crowdfunding
f. Venture capital
g. Angel investors

10. **Select your location.** As you search for a location, conduct your preliminary business in your residence. Considerations for locations:

    a. Residence
    b. Co-work Space
    c. Short term lease

11. **Outsource Accounting.** Hire an accounting to keep your financial records in order.
12. **Create an exit plan.** At the forefront, it is important to create an exit strategy. If you determine entrepreneurship is not for you, a plan of action is in place. This does not mean you plan to fail. It means you have a plan. Can you sell the business? Do you have employees to consider? Do you have bank loans to be repaid? Will you start another business? Will you take a job to cover your business debt?

*For more details refer to the U.S. Small Business Administration at https://www.sba.gov/business-guide/10-steps-start-your-business/

Mini Module

Who Wants To Be An Entrepreneur?

Many of us have thought about owning a business. Perhaps you work at the front desk of a hotel and you think about how much more efficient the operation would be if you owned it. Perhaps you manage a restaurant franchise and you think about the changes you would implement if you owned the establishment. Well, today might be your day. With your knowledge, experience, and a small investment, you can be on your way. Do you truly have the determination and the motivation to take the entrepreneur express? Let's find out.

1. Are you always looking for opportunities?
2. Were you a young hustler?
3. Will consumers buy what you are selling?
4. Is there a demand for your product or service?
5. Do you seek knowledgeable advisors for feedback?
6. Do you connect with individuals who are smarter than you?
7. Do you read blogs, books, and articles, subscribe to business newsletters to improve your skills?
8. Can you motivate yourself to follow through?
9. Do you wake up excited about what you do?
10. Do you embrace change?
11. Are you willing to step outside of your comfort zone?
12. Do you look for outlets to plug into because you realize there is no such thing as spare time?
13. Do you depend on a calendar because you value time and don't want to waste it?

If you answered yes to at least nine of the thirteen questions, you might have the determination on the inside to take the Entrepreneurial Express.

The Entrepreneur Examination

Which side will the dial of the compass land according to your characteristics? Circle one choice under column A or B to determine if you have the characteristics of an entrepreneur or a non-entrepreneur.

A. Entrepreneur   or   **B. Non-Entrepreneur**

A. Entrepreneur		B. Non-Entrepreneur
Willing to come out of your comfort zone	or	Not willing to take a risk
Your insecurities cause you to work smarter	or	Insecurities cause you to work harder
You are confident in your ability	or	You are not sure of your ability
You learn from failing	or	Fear of failing holds you back
You enjoy being around smart people	or	You feel inadequate around smart people

Did you have more under A. or B.? List your final answer below.

Final Characteristic _____

> *Commit your works to the Lord and*
> *your plans will be established.*
> (Proverbs 16:3, NASB)

CHAPTER 5

THE S.S.P. (STRATEGIC SPENDING PLAN)

Cruise Control

A governor is a device that acts as a speed limiter on fuel-injected engines. Briggs and Stratton Manufacturing company produces governors that allow automobiles to cruise at a certain speed without exceeding the recommended speed limit. Creating and following a Strategic Spending Plan allows you to put a governor on your MoneyCycle to keep your finances on cruise control. The Strategic Spending Plan will help keep you from exceeding your spending limit- thus meeting your financial objectives consistently. *(see the Strategic Spending Plan).*

Break it down! What is the Strategic Spending Plan?

A successful S.S.P consists of both a strategic plan and a budget for spending. The strategic plan lays out the directions and goals, along with a plan of action to achieve those goals. The S.S.P creates long-range financial goals spanning over one year. It also includes shorter intervals to measure success during the process. The S.S.P. intends to develop a plan which supports a long-range vision for financial independence, wealth, or financial goals you desire to achieve. Implementing the S.S.P will allow you to create a spending plan which will help you make wise money management decisions. It safeguards you, providing enough money for the things you need, along with the things that are important to you. Following the S.S.P. can get you out of debt, help you stay out of debt, and help you to work your way towards the financial independence you desire and deserve.

The Good, The Bad, And The Ugly

You must know where you are to determine where you are going. Let's get right down to the raw truth. The truth might be ugly or it might not be as ugly as you think. Either way, you need to know the truth to put yourself in the best financial position possible. Just think, you already started and you are on your way. At this point, you want to grow. This means you need to know where you are to determine how far you have come, where you would like to go, and the path to travel to get there. The S.S.P. in the next few pages will help you understand what you are working with or without.

> "Embrace the good,
> Eliminate the bad,
> Eradicate the ugly."
> *Dr. Karen Totten White*

The goal is to embrace the good, eliminate the bad, and eradicate the ugly.

The Good. Debts are paid on time each month. An emergency fund and a retirement fund are established. No matter how large or small, you have one.

The Bad. Debts are paid, but not on time. Debts are delinquent, you are making your June payment in July. You don't have an emergency fund. However, you do have a retirement plan through your employer.

The Ugly. Debts are paid when you can if you can. You avoid creditor calls. You have excessive debt. You don't have an emergency fund. You may or may not have a retirement plan through your employer.

The Strategic Spending Plan will put you in control of your debt instead of your debt controlling you. Your S.S.P. will provide a clear snapshot of how much money you have coming in, how much money is going out, and where your money is going. This snapshot allows you to determine where you can make trade-offs to find extra cash, increase your inbound cash flow, and increase your residual income. Some of these methods are listed in the "Invest in Yourself" and "Financial Fitness" chapters. You are about to take a major first step in accomplishing larger financial goals. With the S.S.P. in place, you gain a clear picture of how to do what you need to do to reach financial independence. It allows you to review your spending habits, determine what can be decreased or eliminated, and determine which funds can be shifted into other categories. You may discover some of the weekly or monthly debts you incur may be a want and not a need. There is a difference. A need is something you must have. A want is something you would like to have, but don't need. Therefore, once you evaluate your debt, you can determine which expenses can be eliminated. The extra cash you find can be moved to an emergency fund or applied to pay off another debt earlier than expected. The elimination of a debt or discovery of funds is a reason to celebrate.

Separation: A Need or a Want?

Around the age of sixteen, I passed my driver's license test. Of course, this meant I *needed* a car. With great enthusiasm, I informed my dad, "Dad, I passed my test. I have my driver's license! When can we go get my car?" My dad was truly the epitome of the tall, dark, and handsome. When he smiled his pearly white teeth and contagious laugh made me want to reciprocate with a smile. His bold, sandalwood fragrance could consume a ballroom. His mountain of charisma towered to 5'11" and made me feel like I was in a cozy, comfort zone. Yet, on that day, I thought I had asked a simple question. To me, it felt like I might have been asking for a pair of Moxi Lolly Blue Beach Bunny Roller Skates. Well, there is a first time for everything and this was it for me. He turned to me, smiled, and said "Good job on your test, but I'm not buying you a car right now." The sound of "no" echoed like a tractor-trailer screeching as it slammed on brakes leaving long black marks on the highway. I did not understand him saying, "No." I only asked for a car. I was emotionally crushed. I had no idea he would deny my simple request. Had I fallen from his grace? I was the apple of his eye. Yet, it appeared I had fallen from grace, like a crisp, green apple falling from the top branch of a towering tree. I thought to myself, "Does he really mean no. It's just a car. It has four wheels just like the Moxi Lolly Blue Beach Bunny Roller Skates. How could he say no to my *need*."

My dad understood I *wanted* a car. But he knew, I did not *need* a car. I did not understand how much money was involved in my request. The car, tags, decals, oil changes, tires, regular maintenance, not to mention gas and insurance was a pricey combo for a sixteen-year-old. Did I get over it? You better believe I did. The village came through. My Papa had a White 2-door 1970 Ford Maverick, a Golden Brown 2-door 1976 Cadillac Eldorado Biarritz Coupe, and a Tan 2-door 1980 Chevrolet Chevette Hatchback parked outside of our home. He drove a car, my mom drove a car, and I could drive whatever car was left parked in the driveway. All I needed to say was, "Papa, I *need* to use a car, which one can I drive?" I could ride all day putting $2 worth of gas in the Ford and the Chevrolet. It took $3 for the Cadillac. I did not need a car. I wanted transportation. My dad saying 'no' allowed me to realize what I needed had already been provided for me, as always. Sometimes we have what we need. We just need to assess the situation, adjust accordingly, and be grateful as we navigate our journey. At sixteen, I learned the difference between a need and a want.

> *And my God will supply all your needs according to His riches in glory in Christ Jesus.* (Philippians 4:19, NASB)

Creating A Strategic Spending Plan. The S.S.P.

Financial success doesn't happen overnight for most individuals. It is the result of making a wise choice on major and minor financial decisions. The Strategic Spending Plan allows you to visually create your personal, financial road map. This allows you to determine where you are spending your money, how much you are spending, how much residual income you have, if you are overspending, where you can decrease some spending, and more. The S.S.P. will also assist you in building a budget, increasing your emergency savings, building investment accounts, and eliminating debt.

Instead of paying interest, you will earn interest. How does that sound to you? Stop paying and get paid. This will result in you building a solid financial foundation for long-term success to financial independence.

Completing the charts in the pages will allow you to put your debt in perspective. The goal is to move forward at a constant pace. Remember, this will not happen overnight. Whatever your financial situation, it can be fixed or improved. Knowledge is power. The MoneyCycle empowers you by providing guidance and knowledge to be successful on your journey to financial independence. I have confidence in you. I need you to have confidence in yourself.

> *The plans of the diligent lead surely to advantage,*
> *but everyone who is hasty comes surely to poverty.*
> (Proverbs 21:5, NASB)

Are We There Yet?

We have reached a major pitstop. It's time to stop, rest up, fuel up, check the oil, check the tires, and all other maintenance involved when you are traveling. The road maintenance in this journey involves gathering the data to complete your Strategic Spending Plan. If you answered the questions in the first four chapters, then you should be able to determine your financial goals. Completing the charts in the S.S.P. will put your plans in to action to achieve your financial goals.

Mini-Module:

Strategic Spending Plan:

The Strategic Spending Plan is a "living document." This means it will be modified over time according to the changes in your lifestyle. You might go over budget in a few categories for some months. That's okay. You may be under budget in other categories. That's great. Just remember to assess the situation and adjust accordingly. You will eventually find a rhythm and learn how to make adjustments smoothly. Establish your money space, make an appointment with yourself to update your S.S.P. to remain on target towards your goal of financial independence.

To get started:

- Add your actual expenses and income from the previous month
- Subtract the total of your expenses from the total of your monthly income
- Set this month's spending targets
- Subtract this month's spending targets from last month's actuals to determine (+/-) you are spending in each category

Refer to the S.S.P. worksheet throughout the month to track your spending. At the end of the month, enter the actual cost of each expense and compare those figures to your spending targets.

Strategic Spending Plan

MONTHLY EXPENSES					
Housing	Last Month's Actual $ Spent	This Month's Spending Target	Estimated Difference	This Month's Actual $	Actual Difference
Mortgage/Rent					
Second Mortgage					
Maintenance					
Homeowners/ Renters Insurance					
HOA/Other fees					
Other					
Other					
Other					
Housing Subtotal					

Strategic Spending Plan

MONTHLY EXPENSES					
Utilities	Last Month's Actual $ Spent	This Month's Spending Target	Estimated Difference	This Month's Actual $	Actual Difference
Electricity					
Gas					
Water					
Trash Service					
Cell Phone/ Landline					
Cable/Satellite					
Internet Service					
Other					
Other					
Other					
Utilities Subtotal					

Strategic Spending Plan

MONTHLY EXPENSES					
Transportation	**Last Month's Actual $ Spent**	**This Month's Spending Target**	**Estimated Difference**	**This Month's Actual $**	**Actual Difference**
Car Payment					
Car Payment					
Car Payment					
Fuel					
Maintenance					
Parking/Tolls					
Other					
Transportation Subtotal					
Food	**Last Month's Actual $ Spent**	**This Month's Spending Target**	**Estimated Difference**	**This Month's Actual $**	**Actual Difference**
Groceries					
Eating Out					
Other:					
Other:					
Other:					
Food Subtotal					

Strategic Spending Plan

MONTHLY EXPENSES					
Clothing	Last Month's Actual $ Spent	This Month's Spending Target	Estimated Difference	This Month's Actual $	Actual Difference
Adult					
Adult					
Children					
Children					
Dry Cleaning					
Other:					
Other:					
Clothing Subtotal					
Health	Last Month's Actual $ Spent	This Month's Spending Target	Estimated Difference	This Month's Actual $	Actual Difference
Medications					
Contacts/ Supplies					
Gym Membership					
Other:					
Other:					
Health Subtotal					

Strategic Spending Plan

MONTHLY EXPENSES					
Personal Expense	Last Month's Actual $ Spent	This Month's Spending Target	Estimated Difference	This Month's Actual $	Actual Difference
Alimony/Child Support					
Child Care					
Emergency Saving					
Certificate of Deposit					
Money Market					
Stock					
Education					
Life Insurance					
Charitable Contributions					
Barber/Beauty Shop					
Vacations					
Recreation / Hobbies					
Alcohol/Tobacco					
Entertainment					
Pet Maintenance					
Other:					
Other:					
Personal Expense Subtotal					

Strategic Spending Plan

MONTHLY EXPENSES					
Personal Debt	Last Month's Actual $ Spent	This Month's Spending Target	Estimated Difference	This Month's Actual $	Actual Difference
Credit Card Payment					
Credit Card Payment					
Credit Card Payment					
Credit Card Payment					
Credit Card Payment					
Credit Card Payment					
Student Loan					
Student Loan					
Loan Payment					
Personal Debt Subtotal					

Strategic Spending Plan

TOTAL MONTHLY EXPENSES					
Add the sub-total to each category	Last Month's Actual $ Spent	This Month's Spending Target	Estimated Difference	This Month's Actual $	Actual Difference
Housing					
Utilities					
Transportation					
Food					
Clothing					
Health					
Personal Expense					
Personal Debt					
Total Monthly Expenses					

Strategic Spending Plan

MONTHLY INCOME					
	Last Month's Actual $	This Month's Projected Income	Estimated Difference	This Month's Actual Income	Actual Difference
Net Monthly Salary (Actual take home pay)-Self					
Net Monthly Salary (Actual take home pay)-Partner					
Part-Time Job					
Part-Time Job					
Tips					
Bonuses					
Retirement					
Retirement					
Child Support					
Social Security Payment					
TANF					
Other:					
Other:					
Other:					
Total Monthly Income					

Total Actual Monthly Income $

Total Actual Monthly Expenses   **(minus)-** $

***Extra Cash for Savings and
Paying down other debts.***   **(equals)=** $

If you have a negative number look back at your expenses to determine where you can decrease your spending. For example, eating out. Enter your new spending targets and the amount saved in the appropriate columns. For example, say you want to trim you're eating out expenses from $350 to $250, enter $250 in "This Month's Spending Target" column and $100 in the "Estimated Difference" column.

If you have a positive number, consider adding it to your savings or paying down high-interest debts. You may still want to review your expenses and look for possible cuts to help you pay down your debt or reach your savings goals faster.

DR. KAREN TOTTEN WHITE

Strategic Spending Plan

MONTHLY SAVINGS/INVESTMENTS					
Savings/ Investment	Last Month's Actual $	This Month's Projected Income	Estimated Difference	This Month's Actual Income	Actual Difference
Emergency Savings					
Vacation Savings					
Certificate of Deposit					
Individual Retirement Accounts					
Personal Savings					
Personal Savings					
Stock					
Money Market					
Investments					
Other:					
Other:					
Total Monthly Savings					

Small Change = Big Savings

A few modifications in your budget can increase your savings and investments over time. If you reduced your spending in several categories, add up the "Estimated Difference" column and multiply that number by 12. This is how much more money you could save over a year if you are constant with your spending targets.

Estimated Difference Total　　　　　$ ⬜

X12 ⬜

Total Savings　　　(equals)　　$ ⬜

Strategic Spending Plan

RESIDUAL INCOME					
	Last Month's Actual $	This Month's Projected Income	Estimated Difference	This Actual Income	Actual Difference
Total Monthly Income					
Total Monthly Expenses					
Total Residual Income					

Total Actual Monthly Income $

Total Actual Monthly Expenses   (minus)- $

Residual Income for Savings and Paying down other debts.   (equals)= $

CONCLUSION

According to CNN Money, being financially independent means your income from your investments alone will be enough to cover all your expenses. The choices you make today will determine your destiny tomorrow. Everyone has an opportunity to make money. It is possible, it can be done, and you can do it. The keys to mastering the MoneyCycle include:

- **Making money.** This means income originates from a source.
- **Multiplying money.** This involves using your money to make money.
- **Maintaining money.** This involves preserving funds to create generational wealth.

Money does not and shall not discriminate based on race, color, religion (creed), gender, gender expression, age, national origin (ancestry), disability, marital status, sexual orientation, or military status. It's up to you to make it happen for yourself. Focus on what you can control. Focus on what you can change. Focus on your personal journey to financial independence. It is about learning as you travel. It is about teaching the next generation what you learned including the good, the bad and the ugly. It is about celebrating your victories in little milestones. It is about enjoying the scenery along your voyage as you travel towards financial independence.

REFERENCE

Bach, N. Millions of Amerians Are One Missed Paycheck Away From Poverty, Report Say. January 2019. http://fortune.com/2019/01/29/americans-liquid-asset-poor-propserity-now-report/

Bahney, Anna. *How to become financially independent in 5 years.* June, 2017. https://money.cnn.com/2017/06/06/retirement/retire-5-years/index.html

Beattie, A. *How to Increase Your Disposable Income.* April 2018. https://www.investopedia.com/articles/pf/07/disposable_income.asp

Carter, S. *30% of Americans are 'constantly' stressed out about money-but you don't have to be.* March 2018. CNBC. https://www.cnbc.com/2018/03/19/30-percent-of-americans-are-stressed-out-about-money-constantly.html

Graves, D. E., *What is the Madder with Lydia's Purple? A Reexamination of the Purpurarii in Thyatira and Philippi.* January, 2017. https://www.researchgate.net/publication/321241274_What_is_the_Madder_with_Lydia's_Purple_A_Reexamination_of_the_Purpurarii_in_Thyatira_and_Philippi

Kleinhandler, D. *Generational Wealth: Who do 7% of Families Lose Their Wealth in the 2ⁿᵈ Generation?* https://www.nasdaq.com/article/generational-wealth-why-do-70-of-families-lose-their-wealth-in-the-2nd-generation-cm1039671

Love money Staff. *20 Lottery Winners Who Blew It All.* December 2017. https://www.msn.com/en-us/money/personalfinance/20-lottery-winners-who-blew-it-all/ss-BBGHB3D

Sine, R. *Beyond 'White Coat Syndrome.' Fear of doctors and tests can hin-der preventative health care.* https://www.webmd.com/anxiety-panic/features/beyond-white-coat-syndrome#1

White, K. (2012). *A Self-exam to become Financially Fit.* Dan River Emerge! Summer 2012 p. 30-31. http://issuu.com/showcasemagazine/docs/emerge_summer_2012_web/31?e=0

www.annualcreditreport.com

https://www.biblegateway.com/

https://www.calculatorsoup.com/

https://www.gettyimages.com/landing/pa-preview/expanded/18458

https://www.sba.gov/

Made in the USA
Columbia, SC
17 December 2020